1996

Outsider Features

OUTSIDER FEATURES

American Independent Films of the 1980s

RICHARD K. FERNCASE

Contributions to the Study of Popular Culture, Number 52

GREENWOOD PRESS
Westport, Connecticut • London

Library of Congress Cataloging-in-Publication Data

Ferncase, Richard K.
    Outsider features : American independent films of the 1980s /
    Richard K. Ferncase.
        p. cm.—(Contributions to the study of popular culture,
    ISSN 0198–9871 : no. 52)
    Includes bibliographical references and index.
    ISBN 0–313–27607–2 (alk. paper)
    1. Motion pictures—United States. 2. Low budget films.
    I. Series.
    PN1993.5.U6F44   1996
    791.43'75'0973—dc20   95–52798

British Library Cataloguing in Publication Data is available.

Library of Congress Catalog Card Number: 95–52798
ISBN: 0–313–27607–2
ISSN: 0198–9871

First published in 1996

Greenwood Press, 88 Post Road West, Westport, CT 06881
An imprint of Greenwood Publishing Group, Inc.

Printed in the United States of America

The paper used in this book complies with the
Permanent Paper Standard issued by the National
Information Standards Organization (Z39.48–1984).

10 9 8 7 6 5 4 3 2 1

For Nancy

"Un art auquel la jeunesse ne peut participer librement est con-
damne d'avance. Il importe que la camera devienne un stylographe
et que chacun puisse traduire son ame dans le style visuel."

"An art form that young people cannot practice freely is doomed
in advance. It is essential that the camera become a pen that
everyone can use to express themself in this visual medium."

Jean Cocteau, "En faveur du 16
millimetres." *Du Cinematographe,*
Pierre Belfond, ed. Paris: 1973;
London: Marion Boyars, 1988: 66.

Contents

Acknowledgments

Thankfully, the writing of a book requires considerably less collaborative effort than the making of a film. Nonetheless, I could not have put this together without the help of numerous individuals. I would like to thank Lizzie Borden, John Sayles, and Errol Morris for taking the time to speak to me about their projects, as well as Ethan Coen and Steven Soderbergh, who were thoughtful enough to return my correspondence. Thanks to Klaus Eder and Debbi Zimmerman, who provided key bits of information over the Internet, and Nancy Hoegler, who helped proofread final copies of the manuscript. Lastly, I thank Nina Pearlstein and Dr. James Sabin, who stayed committed to the project throughout its six years of development.

Preface

In an article in the program for the 1989 U.S. (now Sundance) Film Festival, British critic and filmmaker Peter Wollen compared the burgeoning independent movement in contemporary American filmmaking to the development of the *Société des Artistes Indépendants* in mid-nineteenth-century France.[1] This group, formed by innovative artists whose works had been rejected by the official *Salon* (an annual exhibition held by the traditional *Académe*), organized and exhibited their works in an alternative exhibition they called the *Salon des Indépendants*, a development considered by many to mark the beginning of modernism in the visual arts. "To my mind," Wollen wrote, "independence comes from a working through of rejection rather than a search for acceptance." These words rang with peculiar irony in the final year of a decade that saw unprecedented critical and public acceptance of numerous independent films. Some of them, including *She's Gotta Have It*, *sex, lies, and videotape*, and *Roger & Me*, were embraced by mainstream audiences, literally making millions for their respective creators Spike Lee, Steven Soderbergh, and Michael Moore. The year also was a watershed for the small Park City independent showcase, which saw its attendance double by the mid-1990s, and even more significantly, drew the rapt attention of both Hollywood and the global film community at large. Independents continued to find the Motion Picture Academy a hard nut to crack, but they would regularly take top honors at the Cannes International Film Festival. One-time upstarts such as Soderbergh, Joel and Ethan Coen,

David Lynch, and Quentin Tarantino soon became envied filmmakers. The once-humble independent film had come of age—but had independent filmmakers abandoned their maverick origins, attracted by Hollywood's riches and fame?

Much has been written about this independent film movement that came of age in the 1980s, with many observers acknowledging these independent works as the most exciting motion pictures made in the last twenty years. Some referred to an "American New Wave," comparing the American indie filmmakers to the directors of France's landmark *Nouvelle Vague*: Godard, Truffaut, Resnais, and others. Inevitably, skeptics raised a thorny question: Was independent filmmaking really an alternative to the Hollywood production mill, or was it simply an eager filmmaker's "audition" for the movie industry—a director's rite of passing, as it were—before being plucked up by the starmaking machinery? As David Ansen cautioned in 1987, "Visionary filmmaking can be another name for cut-rate financing, and hope for a reformation that could change the nature of Hollywood might be just another creative mirage. . . . A little film 'from the heart' called *Rocky* was supposed to teach the studios that less is more. They learned a lesson all right, but it wasn't 'Small is beautiful.' " [2]

The independent label, applied to all types of films, from the fringe experimental works of Yvonne Rainer to the decidedly mainstream offerings of Clint Eastwood, has clearly lost its meaning. A more precise term—*specialty film*—has been coined to describe a type of independent film that differs from the common low-budget commercial film and the exploitation feature. In their survey of independently produced films, *Off-Hollywood: The Making and Marketing of American Specialty Films*, Peter Rosen and David Hamilton explain:

> Specialty films—feature-length by definition in that they are intended to have a life in theatrical distribution—reflect the personal vision of the filmmakers, who retain complete control over their projects. However unique, specialty films share a common humanism and are neither racist, sexist nor exploitative; this is a key distinguishing difference between independently produced, low-budget genre films. A relatively low production budget is another defining characteristic of specialty films. Another feature common to specialty films is the nature of their audiences, which tends to be an older, more highly educated segment of the moviegoing public. The specialty audience is typically more serious and sophisticated in its filmgoing than the general consumer audience, tending to seek out "films"—as opposed to movies—which offer an exquisitely realized or unusual aesthetic or dramatic experience, perhaps including some psychological, cultural or socio-historical in-

sight. While specialty films have traditionally been a niche market, there is nothing inherent in them to prevent their potential breaking out to a larger audience.[3]

A more appropriate term might be the *outsider feature*, describing feature-length films by relatively unknown filmmakers often trained in film schools. These films may vary in budget, but they generally cost significantly less than $1 million, often less than $200,000. Often they are shot in 16mm format. They generally feature no "name" actors and tend to be based on scripts written by the filmmakers themselves. Many of the films examined in this book emerged from seeming nowhere and, ironically, made celebrities of their makers, effectively ending their outsider status.

All the films discussed in this volume were funded and shot independently, often in the 16mm format, without studio assistance. Some of the filmmakers discussed, notably Jim Jarmusch, continue to retain relative independence (and, in the case of Jarmusch, actual ownership of the films' negatives as well) by eschewing the usual studio financing, instead seeking financing overseas. Many have since gone on to make films with funding from the majors—Universal (Spike Lee), Orion (Susan Seidelman), Columbia (Ethan and Joel Coen)—as well as under the auspices of smaller firms such as Miramax (Lizzie Borden) and Gramercy (Steven Soderbergh). A few have struggled to find a suitable balance between independence and studio support (Wayne Wang, Michael Moore). While most of these directors now work with studios and can no longer qualify as being truly "independent," all were outsiders when they made the films discussed in this book. Whether it is advisable, or even feasible, for one to remain steadfastly "independent" as a filmmaker of mainstream features is subject for debate, though it would seem that continued success in the American film industry is inevitably contingent upon some kind of relationship with the studios and distributors that now own or control most of the nation's exhibition houses.

This book examines the realization of some personal dreams that, with few connections and little money, succeeded beyond all imaginings, in a heady and ephemeral season of innocence, idealism, and—yes—independence.

NOTES

1. p. 3.
2. David Ansen, "Hollywood Goes Independent: The Underground Becomes the Overground as 'Indies' Make More Movies than the Studios," *Time*, April 6, 1987, p. 64.
3. David Rosen, with Peter Hamilton, *Off-Hollywood: The Making and Marketing of American Specialty Films* (New York: Grove Weidenfeld, 1990),

pp. xvii–iii. Interestingly, the book was re-released under the title *Off-Hollywood: The Making and Marketing of Independent Films*, a change that would indicate that the publisher or authors were no longer comfortable with the term "specialty films" or else assumed that the term "independent films" had become a buzz word with built-in reader recognition.

CHAPTER 1

Introduction:
Intruders in the Enchanters' Domain

A Brief History of American Outsider Cinema

Independent filmmaking is not a recent phenomenon in the history of American motion pictures; it is as old as the medium itself. As long as the powers that be have exerted control over the machinery of filmmaking and the distribution of movies, there have been outsiders scheming and clamoring to gain access.

When Thomas Edison patented assistant W.K.L. Dickson's extraordinary motion picture camera, he made certain that no others would be able to purchase one. Although films produced by the Edison studio were rudimentary at best, they were the only motion pictures produced for several years, as Edison jealously guarded the invention. The earliest moving pictures to spring from the new medium, *Fred Ott's Sneeze* (1891) and *The Kiss* (1896), were little more than simple demonstrations of the revolutionary technology. Oddly, Edison did not consider the motion picture as a theater medium—his films could be viewed only in the coin-operated peep shows he licensed to penny arcade and carnival operators.

UPSTARTS AND USURPERS

After studying Edison's device, the Lumière brothers of France fashioned their own camera-projector, the Cinematograph, and held the first public projected screening of a film in 1895. Their films (they called them *actualités*), which captured real-life events, caused a sensation in Paris. The Lumières also wanted to retain control over their successful invention, and refused to sell a camera to fellow Frenchman George Méliès, who was interested in the new technology. Méliès, a professional magician, instead had a camera specially made and began making films with a vision quite unlike that of Edison or the Lumières. Films such as *A Trip to the Moon* (1903) were meticulously choreographed feats of motion picture magic. Although Méliès' pictures adhered slavishly to theatrical conventions, they were the first to demonstrate the cinema's power for elaborate storytelling.

In the United States, William S. Porter went to work for Edison and made two films that pioneered the naturalistic narrative tradition for the classic American movie: *The Life of an American Fireman* (1903) and *The Great Train Robbery* (1904). In order to protect his patents and discourage competition, in 1909 Edison gathered together the nine major production companies and formed the Motion Picture Patents Company (MPPC). This monopoly sought to dominate the budding motion picture industry by controlling film stock and equipment, and by intimidating uncooperative exhibitors. The MPPC made a deal with the Eastman Kodak Company to sell its film solely to members of the trust, and refused to do business with exhibitors who screened films produced by non-MPPC members. The company enforced its policies in courts, and sent thugs to destroy equipment and film in scores of studios and theaters. In 1910, independently run cinemas were denied MPPC products until they agreed to a takeover; those that did not comply were driven out of business.

The monolithic control of the MPPC was short-lived. A licensing fee of two dollars per week levied by the MPPC had created widespread dissension among exhibitors. At least forty independent distributors were already producing motion pictures with European film stock and equipment. One of these independents, William Fox, filed suit against the company, and in 1915 the MPPC was declared illegal under the Sherman Anti-Trust Act and ordered to break up. By this time, however, several independents had established a lucrative trade out on the West Coast.

HOLLYWOOD: FROM INDEPENDENT FREEDOM TO STUDIO CONTROL

Much comment has been made about California's sunny climate luring filmmakers from the blustery East. Early entrepreneurs more likely flocked to the West not for mild weather but rather to escape the court orders and goon squads of the Motion Picture Patents Company. Hollywood and the San Fernando Valley were a long way from the MPPC's Pinkerton detectives back east, and the Mexican border was within easy crossing distance just in case officials came calling. Ironically, within a few years a studio system evolved whose influence and power would far exceed that ever attained by the short-lived Motion Picture Patents Company.

By 1914, Hollywood had been created and colonized by the independent filmmakers, largely first- and second-generation immigrants from central Europe. They included Adolf Zukor, Carl Laemmle, Jesse Lasky, Samuel Goldfish, Louis B. Mayer, Marcus Loew, Lewis J. Selznick, William Fox, and the brothers Warner, who founded what were to become Paramount, Universal, Samuel Goldwyn, MGM, Warner Brothers, and Twentieth-Century Fox studios. One of the major developments of this period was the evolution of the feature-length film. Following Adolf Zukor's acquisition of Paramount Film Company in 1917, the studios soon controlled film distribution as well as production. The next step was to buy up movie theaters, thus assuring vertical control and a virtual monopoly of America's motion picture industry. Operating costs as well as profits rose dramatically, as motion picture production came to be controlled both economically and artistically by bankers and businessmen rather than filmmakers.

Dissatisfied with the studios, and in order to produce and distribute their own films independently, leading film talents of the day D. W. Griffith, Charles Chaplin, Mary Pickford, and Douglas Fairbanks joined together in 1919 and formed United Artists (UA). The group prospered in the early twenties, but was later unable to release a sufficient number of films and find enough independent theaters to screen them. It languished for several decades until emerging strong again in the 1950s. (In 1980 the studio was swallowed up by MGM after overextending itself financially with Michael Cimino's megabudget failure, *Heaven's Gate*.)

In a move that recalled the MPPC antitrust litigations twenty-five years earlier, the federal government filed suit against the five major studios in the celebrated 1938 *United States* v. *Paramount Pictures* case. The trials ended in 1948, when the government ruled that the studios' vertical control of the industry constituted a monopoly and ordered them to divest themselves of their theaters. These rulings, commonly known as the Paramount consent decrees, hastened the demise of the studio system. Exhibitors, free from coercive studio practices such as block booking, were now free to show any film they wished, including those produced in Europe. With Hollywood on the decline, the 1950s saw the dawning of a new phenomenon in motion picture history: the independently produced film.

AMERICAN INDEPENDENT ANTECEDENTS

Until the 1950s, the motion picture industry in the United States was virtually dominated by an oligarchy of Hollywood studios that included the five majors—MGM (Loew's), Paramount, Twentieth-Century Fox, Warner Brothers, and RKO—and three minor studios—Universal, Columbia (created by Harry Cohn in 1924), and United Artists. During this period, motion picture production was an assembly-line process, and even directors like Frank Capra were under the thumb of moguls such as Harry Cohn. A few brilliant but profligate *auteurs* such as Stroheim, Sternberg, and Welles emerged, but they were ulimately shunned by the Hollywood community; their films, defying conventional commercial expectations, were often taken from them by the studios and effectively butchered in the quest for profits. Oddly, it was the directors of B-pictures who enjoyed the greatest freedom in terms of creative control over their films.

B-pictures were cheap sixty- to seventy-five-minute movies designed to fill the lesser half of a double bill. A number of substudios emerged in the 1930s to produce these films, including Monogram and Republic. Block booking practices eliminated the threat of competition and ensured the meager prosperity of these studios, known collectively as Poverty Row. Though much B-product was formulaic and hackneyed, a few films of remarkable vision emerged from the B-studios.

EDGAR ULMER

Despite popular belief, directors of B-pictures were not all hacks, a case in point being the recently reevaluated Edgar Ulmer. He was originally an A-picture director, producing some classic films including The *Black Cat* for Universal. Ulmer's career in B-pictures began when Universal attempted to loan him out to make a Shirley Temple movie for Twentieth-Century Fox. Ulmer refused to comply, and Universal fired him. He directed a number of low-budget films for various producers, ending up at the cheapest studio of Poverty Row, Producer's Releasing Corporation. According to film historian Wheeler W. Dixon, "Ulmer was allowed to do whatever he wanted as long as he kept the budgets under $40,000 and shot the film in six to ten days."[1] The rediscovered B-classic *Detour* is a good example of Ulmer's unique vision restrained only by budget. The picture was reportedly shot for $20,000 and used only three sets. *Detour* is remarkable for its uncompromising blend of German expressionism and film noir sensibilities. The tone is one of unremitting existentialist absurdity as the doomed hero struggles to free himself of the events that ensnare and consume him. It is difficult to imagine any major studio releasing a film like *Detour* now, let alone in the postwar climate of 1945.

In the wake of the consent decrees, many of the B-picture studios, which were dependent on block-booking procedures, simply vanished. Those that survived turned to the production of shorter films for television, now siphoning off ever-increasing portions of the moviegoing public. The major studios tried expensive gimmicks such as widescreen and 3–D to regain their audiences, and the average feature-length film grew from ninety minutes to over two hours. Meanwhile, independents were turning out products as quickly and cheaply as possible.

RUSS MEYER

Two notable directors to emerge from the fifties were Russ Meyer and John Cassavetes. Meyer, a onetime army cinematographer who came to be dubbed "King of the Nudies," shot his first film, *The Immoral Mr. Teas*, during four days in 1959 for $24,000. The film, financed in part by the proprietor of a San Francisco strip house, was produced to cash in on the growing popularity of European nudist camp films. As critic Roger Ebert noted with some amusement, these films "were of interest largely because of the actors' difficulties in manipulating bath towels and in standing in front of shrubbery."[2] Meyer reasoned correctly that the rise of *Playboy* magazine had created an audience for a high-quality "skin flick." The mostly improvised *Mr. Teas* centered on an office loaned by Meyer's dentist. It portrayed a false teeth delivery man with a droll affliction: any attractive woman he encountered would appear inexplicably naked. The shock of the nudity was tempered by the nature of Teas's ocular disorder; since what he saw was out of his control, it was okay for the audience to look as well. The film had a long if limited showing (not many theaters were available then even for relatively benign nudie pictures). The *Wall Street Journal* reported that the film spawned "one hundred and fifty imitations within a year—more films than the genre had produced in the previous five decades."[3]

The success of *Mr. Teas* spurred Meyer to crank out several more nudies before moving on to his trademark sex and violence exploitation films of the 1960s. Of them, *Mudhoney* and *Faster, Pussycat! Kill! Kill!* were highly praised by director John Waters, who called them "my *Citizen Kane*."[4] Meyer's later films featured hired screenwriters (among them Tom Wolfe and Roger Ebert), outrageous plot structures, and the usual overendowed leading ladies. In the permissive 1970s, however, his films appeared almost quaint and downright tame when compared to hardcore pornographic fare such as *Deep Throat* and *Bhind the Green Door*. Unlike many independents who ascended the motion picture industry ladder, Meyer continues to produce and direct films himself, casting unknowns in leading roles and filming many of them in his own home.

JOHN CASSAVETES AND *SHADOWS*

John Cassavetes is often called the father of American independent filmmaking. Born in New York on December 9, 1929, of Greek parents, he grew up on Long Island and graduated from the New York Academy of Dramatic Arts in 1953. Cassavetes found work as an actor in numerous films and in 1957 organized a method acting workshop. During a radio interview, Cassavetes proposed a film project constructed around several improvisations conducted in the workshop. His comments attracted $20,000 in contributions from listeners. The film that emerged from the workshop was

Shadows, a $40,000 experimental feature as unlike the "underground" films of its day as it was from Hollywood narrative movies. Shot over a period of two years, the film concerns three black orphan youths, two of whom pass as whites.

Notable for the emphasis on acting over structure, the film makes use of contemporary jazz and street vernacular, taking place almost entirely in a single New York City apartment. The film won the Critic's Award at the 1960 Venice Film Festival, a restrained positive review from the *New York Times*, and a reputation as the first major American response to the French New Wave. It has since become a model of expressive low-budget filmmaking. The relative success of *Shadows* launched the "amateur" directing career of "professional" actor Cassavetes, who siphoned much of his acting pay into financing many of his later films, including *Faces, Husbands, A Woman under the Influence*, and *The Killing of a Chinese Bookie*.

GEORGE ROMERO AND *NIGHT OF THE LIVING DEAD*

A direct descendent of the low-budget horror legacy of directors Roger Corman and Herschell Gordon Lewis, George Romero rose from relative obscurity in Pittsburgh to outdo his predecessors in 1968 with the now-legendary *Night of the Living Dead*. In Romero's own words, it depicted "a mass return from the grave of the recently dead and their need to feed off the flesh and blood of the living." Panned (and inadvertently praised) by *Variety* as "an unrelieved orgy of sadism," *Night of the Living Dead* was to become a model for thousands of imitators over the next thirty years, making it one of the most influential independent films ever produced.[5]

Much of the film's power derives from the low-budget production values. While *Variety* assailed its "amateurism of the first order," critic Stuart Kaminsky wrote, "The crudity of the film, the pseudo–cinema verité use of the camera adds to the impression that what we are seeing is not solely fantasy, but a nightmare firmly fixed in reality."[6]

Appropriately, Romero's knack for exploitation evolved from a background in advertising. His company Latent Image, a producer of industrial films and commercials, teamed with another advertising firm in hopes of producing a low-budget film that would gain Romero entry into Hollywood. Although *Night of the Living Dead* was produced for $114,000, all but $60,000 was deferred until after the film's release, much less than the $90,000 cost of Romero's most costly effort to that date—a Calgon detergent spot.

Predictably, the low-budget film met with initial resistance. AIP (the 'B' studio American International Pictures) decided against distributing it when Romero refused to tack on an upbeat ending. Columbia passed on it as well, deeming the black-and-white picture unmarketable. A Manhattan theater owner finally agreed to distribute the film and premiered it in New York in 1968. It played to an enthusiastic crowd at the Museum of Modern

Art in 1970 and developed a devoted cult following throughout the seventies on the midnight movie circuit, eventually grossing over $50 million.

THE INFLUENCE OF ROGER CORMAN

Although not an independent filmmaker in the strictest sense of the word, Roger Corman nonetheless directed and produced a number of inventive (if slight) B-movies for American International Pictures, wherein he practically rewrote the book on low-budget filmmaking techniques. In 1970, he founded New World Pictures, the largest "independent" producer and distributor in the United States up to that time. His most important contribution lies not in his own cinematic output, however, but in his fostering of many of the greatest American filmmakers of the latter twentieth century. Francis Coppola, Peter Bogdonavitch, Jonathan Demme, Martin Scorsese, Paul Shrader, and John Sayles are but a few directors who began their illustrious careers writing or directing low-budget features for Corman.

Educated at England's Oxford University, Corman went on in the mid-1950s to direct an average of five films a year—many of them monster movies with science-fiction themes and titles such as *It Conquered the World* and *The Wasp Woman*—for James H. Nicholson and Samuel Arkoff's American International Pictures. Many of his movies made during this time were shot in a phenomenal three days, often using the same sets over and over again. His work gradually became more "sophisticated" as he began to make films based on gothic works by Edgar Allan Poe, including *The Pit and the Pendulum* and *The Raven*. He also made the occasional biting satire—for example, *Bucket of Blood*—that skewered the artistic pretensions of the then-current Beat movement.

Corman produced movies in various genres from westerns (*Gunslinger*) to teen films (*Rock All Night*) to gangster fare (*The St. Valentine's Day Massacre*), but he hit his stride in two influential films that spawned a trend sometimes referred to as the "youth" or "counterculture" film: *The Trip*, which depicted psychedelic drug use and its consequences, and *The Wild Angels*, which updated the biker film genre of the 1950s. Together these films laid the groundwork for one of the most successful independent films to date: Dennis Hopper's *Easy Rider*.

THE SUCCESS OF *EASY RIDER*

A $375,000 independent film that combined the rebellious antiestablishment sensibilities of *The Trip* and the outlaw tradition of *The Wild Angels* with a quasi-political countercultural perspective, *Easy Rider* galvanized the growing "youth movement," astonishing traditional Hollywood as it grossed over $50 million in box office receipts. The movie was produced by

Dennis Hopper and Peter Fonda independently of Corman, but it clearly bore his influence. A cynical B road picture about two boorish and inarticulate hippies who incur much derision from the many backwoods folk they encounter on a journey across the United States to New Orleans' Mardi Gras, *Easy Rider* garnered surprisingly widespread critical praise in 1969 and won a "Best New Director" award at Cannes for Dennis Hopper. The picture has dated considerably since its debut in 1969; in retrospect, its widespread popularity seems due in large degree to the associative effect of its dynamic, highly evocative soundtrack of popular rock songs. The power of popular music as a score was a phenomenon duly noted by subsequent filmmakers and reused to great effect in such films as *American Graffiti* and *The Big Chill*. As the mood of the times began to change again in the seventies, Hollywood was unable to successfully capitalize on the youth movement. Ironically, Hopper too would prove unable to fulfill the promise of his directing debut in such subsequent films as *The Last Movie*. His film career languished throughout the seventies until a role in Coppola's *Apocalypse Now* brought him back to public attention as a popular character actor.[7]

INDEPENDENT FILM IN THE SEVENTIES

> It was like the other ideologies that failed, like communism or something. It's a great idea and you can believe in it—it's very glorious to run up the steps of the proscenium bearing a red flag, but then the bureaucracy takes over. In that case, the idea was that all of these young filmmakers were going to be able to express themselves, and they were going to have, be filled with great ideas that would change the world and give us great works of art, when in fact filmmakers had no great ideas at all, or any ideas at all for the most part, and only gave us greater explosions.
>
> John Milius[8]

Much has been written about the first generation of film school–educated directors that came of age in the late sixties and early seventies: the so-called movie brats. Many observers thought that this was the generation that would change Hollywood in the wake of the studio system's final dissolution. For a brief time, it looked like the commercial interests of Hollywood and the personal aesthetic visions of these new young filmmakers were converging to create a new "golden age" of American cinema. Indeed, for a while during the early seventies (which some hailed as a "Hollywood Renaissance"), upstart directors were creating some of the most intelligent and thought-provoking work in decades: *Five Easy Pieces, The Last Picture Show, Harold and Maude, M*A*S*H, The Candidate*. The trend was not destined to last, however. By 1977, the brats, who had made some interesting personal films in their infancy, now dazzled Hollywood with their abilities to zero in on audience desires with blockbuster pictures such as *The Godfather*, *Jaws*, and *Star Wars*. The huge profits reaped by these films changed the expectations Hollywood would have for future projects, and effectively sounded the death knell for the kind of small pictures that touched a generation early in the decade. It was no longer enough to make a $2 million picture that earned $4 million. Now the game plan was to make fewer big-budget movies that reaped tens of millions in profit. Directors liberated from the back lot to capture the realism of shooting on location found themselves sequestered in the sound stage once again, for the new fantasy entertainments demanded increasingly sophisticated illusion and artifice that could be created only in the controlled environment of the studio. Ironically, even Francis Coppola, who had made the most lucrative film up to that time with *The Godfather*, had trouble generating much interest stateside in his small film about a guilt-ridden sound recording expert that he called *The Conversation*. The film won the Palme d'Or at Cannes, but went unnoticed in his own country.

While the film brats were busy making movies for the major studios, other trends in independent moviemaking were developing far off the beaten Hollywood track, including the emergence of the "blaxploitation" picture, the women's independent film, and the cult movie.

The revolutionary mood of the late 1960s fostered a filmmaking movement by African-American directors who explored African-American themes. Films such as Robert Downey's satirical *Putney Swope*, Gordon Park's *The Learning Tree* and Ossie Davis's *Cotton Comes to Harlem* created a niche for African-American filmmakers and their audiences, but none was as audacious as Melvin Van Peebles's *Sweet Sweetback's Baadasssss Song*, which prefigured a trend toward exploitation, the so-called blaxploitation film. Many of these, such as Park's *Shaft* and *Super-Fly*, mixed interracial coupling with profusely exaggerated violence, thereby winning an enthusiastic audience. Like many other trends born in the sixties, this one did not last, and by the mid-seventies the era of the black film was over. It would be more than ten years before African-American filmmakers would make waves to rock Hollywood.

THE CULT FILM

Perhaps the most exciting trend in outsider cinema came in the form of the cult film, also known as the midnight movie, as most of them screened after 12 o'clock at night in repertory theaters when the featured screenings had ended. The cult film category includes offensive, graphic horror movies such as *The Night of the Living Dead* and *The Texas Chainsaw Massacre*, campy kitsch parodies such as *Dark Star* and the studio-funded *The Rocky Horror Picture Show*, and truly bizarre, surrealistic outings such as *El Topo*, *Pink Flamingos*, and *Eraserhead*. The cult film found its precedent in scandalous early works of forgotten Hollywood directors such as Todd Browning, whose circus exposé *Freaks* was vehemently denounced in its day, only to be resurrected in the 1970s as a gothic classic. Its primal power sprang from a frankly simplistic storyline that contrasted the gentle humanity of sideshow freaks with the ugly brutality of their able-bodied employers. Lurid B-movies from bygone days that purported to reveal the horrors of drugs (such as *Reefer Madness* and *Cocaine Fiends*) proved popular with college audiences, who were often inebriated by the very substances lambasted in the pictures.

For whatever its other merits, George Romero's *Night of the Living Dead* succeeded in kicking off a virtual low-budget horror boom that continued throughout the seventies. One of its most infamous imitators turned out to be an even more nauseating picture, Tobe Hooper's *The Texas Chainsaw Massacre*, which amassed an ardent cult following and found entry into New York City's prestigious Museum of Modern Art film collection. From an independent filmmaker's perspective, however, the most nightmarish scenario was not the film's grotesque depictions of cannibal and zombie depravity, but the manner in which its distributor made off with most of the $3 million earned by this $250,000 picture. *Massacre* led to an even more lucrative and influential horror cheapie in 1978 with the release of John Carpenter's *Halloween*. Carpenter had enjoyed modest cult film success with his science-fiction spoof *Dark Star*, but *Halloween* made back $60 million on an $800,000 investment. *Halloween*'s skillful manipulations of film craft drew the respectful praise from numerous critics, including Gene Siskel and Roger Ebert, but ironically it popularized the critically maligned "mad slasher" genre and spawned a plague of inferior exploitation movies. Many of these pictures, including *Friday the 13th* and *Nightmare on Elm Street*, became virtual monsters in their right, giving birth to as many as four sequels and countless other spinoffs each. By 1981, *Variety* reported that slasher films accounted for 60 percent of all domestic film production and placed twenty-five of these among the year's fifty top-grossing pictures.

The most compelling and disturbing horror movie to emerge during this period was not a conventional slasher film at all, but rather an existential meditation on the consequences of procreation coupled with the dehumanizing effects of pestilential industrial decay. The film, David Lynch's *Eraserhead*, transcended all generic categorization and confounded all attempts to describe its exegesis in conventional terms.

David Lynch, originally a painter, got the inspiration for *Eraserhead* while attending art school in Philadelphia. Funded with a grant from the American Film Institute, the film took several years to complete before premiering at midnight (appropriately) at the Los Angeles International Film Exposition (FILMEX). The film was excoriated by critics (*Variety* called it "a sickening bad-taste exercise"), but nonetheless it became the definitive cult film in a decade known for its abundance of outré midnight movies.[9]

WOMEN INDEPENDENTS

The women's movement that gained momentum in the seventies had little effect on Hollywood's hiring practices, but a handful of female directors were able to make inroads as independent filmmakers. One, Joan Micklin Silver, ignored the rebuffs of the major studios and with $370,000 raised by her husband, made *Hester Street*, an intelligent and touching turn-of-the-century story about a Jewish immigrant family's struggle in New York's Lower East Side. The film was modestly successful, allowing Silver to make films for Hollywood from a distinctly female perspective—*Between the Lines*, *Chilly Scenes of Winter*, *Crossing Delancy*. The studios gave Silver problems, however, even haggling with her choice of titles for her pictures.

Other woman directors, including Claudia Weill, Martha Coolidge, Joyce Chopra, and Penelope Spheeris, gained a foothold as documentarians, and Weill worked often as a cinematographer after completing a documentary on China for actress Shirley MacLaine. She made her first narrative feature *Girlfriends* for $140,000 in 1978. The film centered on a young woman striving to make it as a photographer in New York, and it became a small landmark for women filmmakers in American cinema. Weill was one of the first women elected to the Motion Picture Academy in 1979, but she stumbled somewhat in her next film, the Jill Clayburgh studio picture *It's My Turn*. The movie was not tremendously successful and Weill never fully regained her creative momentum, working sporadically throughout the eighties. She returned somewhat to form in the late eighties and nineties to work in television on series such as *thirtysomething* (where Melanie Mayron reprised her single photographer role of *Girlfriends*), but her most inspiring work remains her pre-Hollywood feature films.[10]

MOVIE BRATS AND THE RISE OF THE BLOCKBUSTER

> Some say that the director's days of glory ended with *Heaven's Gate*. Personally, I think the turning point may have been the rise of the blockbusters, the super-blockbuster films, the hallmark films. Once studios started seeing a hundred and fifty and two hundred million dollar grosses being possible, the directors turned away from making the profitable smaller pictures. . . . A *Taxi Driver*, a *Hardcore*, a *Five Easy Pieces*, a *Last Picture Show* could not be made today. There's no market for these films today.
>
> Roger Ebert[11]

Despite laudable efforts by independent filmmakers to produce unique and thought-provoking works throughout the 1970s, movie theaters themselves continued to be dominated by studio product. The small "art house" and repertory cinemas that specialized in foreign and American "specialty" films since the beginning of the decade were starting to fall by the wayside, a casualty of the burgeoning "video revolution" of VCRs and cheap, readily available rental videocassettes.

As the 1970s wore on, the content if not the technique of most Hollywood films had declined in quality, thanks in no small part to the rise of the first film school generation of film directors to join the commercial motion picture industry, the so-called movie brats. These directors, including Francis Coppola, George Lucas, Steven Spielberg, and Brian DePalma, infiltrated the Hollywood establishment in the late 1960s and early 1970s with the best intentions, determined to change the way the old guard had run the studios. Instead, perhaps unwittingly, the runaway success of their most celebrated efforts fomented a "blockbuster" mentality within the powers that be. Coppola's *The Godfather* astonished Hollywood with its unprecedented gross profits, followed by Lucas's *American Graffiti* and Spielberg's *Jaws*. These led to even to even bigger spectacles with *Star Wars* and *Close Encounters of the Third Kind*, and the appeal of the blockbuster had firmly ensconced itself into the prevailing Hollywood sensibilities. Francis Ford Coppola and his friend George Lucas may well have wanted to establish an alternative film center apart from corrupt Hollywood, with American Zoetrope and LucasFilm, Ltd., respectively. Coppola's somewhat megalomaniacal desire to be a mogul on the order of Harry Cohn was dashed when his hugely expensive projects failed and forced the sale of his American Zoetrope studios and real estate, and Lucas retreated from directing to assume the role of executive producer who oversaw a great number of projects that had more to do with children's movies than with the adult themes of his youth. Despite DePalma's claims of kinship with Jean Luc Godard and Luis Bunuel, critics generally concurred that his contrived thrillers were strictly poor man's Hitchcock, being all style and little substance. John Milius had some small success with *Big Wednesday*, but was ultimately misled by his own jingoism. The only director of the group to develop and grow with any consistency as an artist was Scorsese, who would go on in the eighties to make some of the most remarkable works of the decade as the most gifted American director of his time.

The blockbuster dream was an endless chain of sorts, one that could not continue without incurring some casualties. The first cracks in the firmament could be seen in Coppola's magnum opus *Apocalypse Now*, originally conceived by John Milius and George Lucas's as a 16mm quasi-documentary of the Vietnam War to be shot on location in Indochina during the actual conflict. The script underwent several changes until production began in the Philippines in 1976. When the film ran up expenditures exceeding $20 million, studio chiefs became nervous, but Coppola appeased them by putting up his own money to keep the production going. Coppola was ultimately exonerated when the film became a cause célèbre and took the

Palme d'Or at Cannes (sharing it with *The Tin Drum*), making him the first director in history to win the top award twice. The film's artistic merit was hotly debated by critics, and though it eventually turned a slim profit, *Apocalypse Now* did not perform in a manner expected of a blockbuster. The would-be prestige film that would rock Hollywood to its foundations with its expensive and highly visible failure would not come until the following year.

THE WOULD-BE BLOCKBUSTER THAT BUSTED UNITED ARTISTS

Though *Apocalypse Now* garnered considerable attention, it had not been the first movie based on the Vietnam War to come out of Hollywood. That honor belonged to *The Deer Hunter*, a film made one year earlier by the relatively unknown director Michael Cimino. The film emerged as a dark horse, taking the 1978 Academy Awards by storm and putting its director Michael Cimino on the map as a new and powerful Young Turk in Hollywood. His next film, however, based on the Johnson County wars that broke out in Montana between cattle ranchers and homesteaders at the turn of the century, defied all conventional logic. Entitled *Heaven's Gate*, it was a western in an era when the genre had all but been left for dead. Even worse, Cimino's profligate perfectionism sent its production costs soaring far beyond the excesses incurred by even *Apocalypse Now*—over $40 million. In this case, however, the bloated production could not be saved; its failure rocked the movie industry and succeeded in bankrupting United Artists, the studio founded by film artists more than half a decade earlier as an independent alternative to the major studios. The very visible failure of one of Hollywood's original seven sisters gave film executives pause, and prompted filmmakers to reconsider their priorities when it came to making films.

A NEW AGE FOR INDEPENDENTS

The climate for independent filmmaking improved incrementally but considerably with the dawn of the eighties. A number of factors materialized early in the decade to spur growth of a relatively new type of American movie, the so-called specialty film. The burgeoning home video rental market that was luring audiences away from the repertory and art house theaters was also creating demand for more movies on video. The major studios, in their characteristic inability to gauge fundamental changes in audience and viewer preferences, were not immediately able to tap this market. Instead, this demand for programming opened a door for independents, which along with the growing popularity and proliferation of film festivals in North America, spurred independent production dramatically. In 1980, one of the most popular of the new festivals of the era, the Los Angeles International Film Exposition (FILMEX), hosted a film that would signal a new era of small, personal films by independent American directors who could rightly call themselves *auteurs*.

NOTES

1. Todd McCarthy and Charles Flynn, eds., *Kings of the B's* (New York: Dutton, 1975), p. 89.

2. Roger Ebert, "Russ Meyer: King of the Nudies," in McCarthy and Flynn, eds., *Kings of the B's* (New York: Dutton, 1975), p. 114.

3. Ibid., p. 114.

4. Scott McDonald, *A Critical Cinema: Interviews with Independent Film-makers* (Berkeley: UC Press, 1988), p. 226.

5. J. Hoberman, with Jonathan Rosenbaum, *Midnight Movies* (New York: Harper & Row, 1983), p. 119.

6. Ibid., p. 122.

7. Hopper gained notoriety for even more offbeat roles in the eighties—for example, David Lynch's *Blue Velvet*.

8. Interview. "The Film School Generation," *American Cinema*, Public Broadcasting System, KCET, Los Angeles, April 23, 1995.

9. J. Hoberman, p. 159.

10. See Barbara Koenig Quart, *Women Directors: The Emergence of a New Cinema* (New York: Praeger, 1988) for an in-depth study of Silver, Weill, Coolidge, Chopra, and other women filmmakers of the 1970s and early 1980s.

11. Roger Ebert, interview. George Hickenlooper, *Reel Conversations* (New York: Citadel 1991), p. 368.

CHAPTER 2

All Together Now:
The Return of the Secaucus Seven
(1980)

USA: Unrated

16mm Color

Running time: 106 minutes

Directed by John Sayles

Cast in credits order:

Bruce MacDonald. . . . . Mike

Maggie Renzi. . . . . Katie

Adam LeFevre. . . . . J.T.

Maggie Cousineau. . . . . Frances

Gordon Clapp. . . . . Chip

Jean Passanante. . . . . Irene

Karen Trott. . . . . Maura

Mark Arnott. . . . . Jeff

David Strathairn. . . . . Ron

John Sayles. . . . . Howie

Marisa Smith. . . . . Carol

Amy Schewel. . . . . Lacey

Carolyn Brooks. . . . . Meg
Eric Forsythe. . . . . Captain
Nancy Mette. . . . . Lee
Betsy Julia Robinson. . . . . Amy
Cora Bennett. . . . . Singer
John Mendillo. . . . . Bartender
Steven Zaitz. . . . . Singer
Brian Johnson. . . . . Norman
Ernie Bashaw. . . . . Officer
Jack LaValle. . . . . Booking Officer
Jessica MacDonald. . . . . Stacey
Benjamin Zaitz. . . . . Benjamin
Jeffrey Nelson. . . . . The Man
Maggie Cousineau-Arndt. . . . . Frances

Cinematography by Austin De Besche
Music by Mason Daring
Written by John Sayles
Edited by John Sayles

> In all my films, I've explored questions of identity and community. In *Secaucus Seven*, the community are these people who are glad to be around others they don't have to explain all their jokes to.
>
> John Sayles[1]

If a single film can mark the beginnings of the contemporary American independent feature, it would arguably be John Sayles's *The Return of the Secaucus Seven*. As one of the first low-budget films since Cassavetes's *Shadows* to seriously address the social and political issues of a generation and win a significant audience, it showed the film community that the small film was indeed alive and well. It is especially noteworthy that Sayles chose not to deal in jokeshop horror, in-crowd artiness, or cult-film formalism for his directorial debut but, rather, to present a probing and witty examination of a group that represented an entire generation of young people. This group of people came of age in the late sixties and in the ensuing seventies and eighties found themselves reevaluating their attitudes concerning sex, politics, society, and the process of aging. In its premiere at the 1980 Los Angeles International Film Exposition (FILMEX), audiences gave the film a standing ovation; the consensus was that *The Return of the Secaucus Seven* was one of the most remarkable films to debut that year.

By regrouping a circle of friends gone separate ways since college, the film tapped a number of themes: friendship and its tenuous balance with love and sexuality, the importance of commitment and responsibility versus independence and spontaneity, and the inevitable changes in perspective and temperament that come with growing older. The viewer is provided a particularly revealing window into the group via an outsider, who is introduced to the friends through his lover. The contrast between the insiders and the newcomer, combined with the efforts of the group members to initiate and acculturate him, bring each character and his or her history into sharp relief for the audience. The marvelous empathy Sayles creates for his characters is largely responsible for the film's success. The masterful use of dialogue and skillful character development is the product of the writer-director's own integrity, vision, and compassion; these traits breathe life into the film.

Sayles acknowledges himself as something of a paradox: a blue-collar man of letters.[2] He was born John Thomas Sayles in 1950 in Schenectady, New York, of Irish-German parents. Sayles attended stately Williams College in Massachusetts, for pragmatic reasons—he didn't know what else to do, and he didn't want to go into the army. By his own account, he took creative writing "because it was always the easiest course. They graded you on poundage, and I wrote long stories, so I got A's in that, which brought my average up to C for my other courses, which I mostly didn't go to."[3]

After graduating in 1972, Sayles worked a number of jobs, including meatpacker, day laborer, and nursing home orderly. He hitchhiked across the country several times, picking up interesting stories along the way that would figure into his short stories, many of which formed the collection entitled *The Anarchist's Convention*. He won an O. Henry Prize for the story "I-80 Nebraska, m. 490–m. 205" in 1975, and wrote his first novel, *Pride of the Bimbos*, in twenty-seven weeks while living on unemployment benefits. His experiences at a sausage factory became the basis for the novel *Union Dues*, which garnered a nomination for a National Book Award.

Sayles spent several summers acting at the Eastern Slope Playhouse in North Conway, New Hampshire, where his strapping physique landed him in roles "playing large retarded people, like Lennie in *Of Mice and Men*, the Indian in *One Flew Over the Cuckoo's Nest*." Difficulties in selling *Union Dues* from the New England hinterlands led to him to acquire an agent. Interested in moviemaking, he submitted a script he'd written about the Chicago "Black Sox" scandal of 1919 and got his first screenwriting job—rewriting the script for a low-budget film called *Piranha* for Roger Corman's New World Pictures. Sayles's screenplay, directed by Joe Dante, was a thinly-veiled *Jaws* rip-off with the titular carnivorous fish developed by the military ultimately wreaking havoc at a summer camp. The film performed well on the horror circuit, and Sayles was soon writing scripts for a number of New World projects, including Dillinger bio-pic *The Lady in Red*, sci-fi epic *Battle Beyond the Stars,* werewolf yarn *The Howling,* and the horror spoof *Alligator.*

Although the basic exploitationist premises of Corman films do not generally inspire philosophical analysis, Sayles was able to imbue the scripts he wrote for the producer with a certain sociopolitical sensibility:

> In *Piranha,* the horror is caused by the military, and there's some kind of awareness, from the characters themselves, that we've been down this river before. . . . [In *Alligator*] my idea was that the alligator eats its way through the whole socio-economic system. It comes out of the sewer in the ghetto, then goes to a middle-class neighborhood, then out to the suburbs, and then to a real kind of high-rent area.[4]

Though Sayles found it possible to work mild political and personal expressions into these by-the-numbers genre films, he yearned to have greater creative control over his work and direct his own films. He pooled the earnings from his scripts and books to finance the making of an audition piece, a film that would show he could write and direct a feature himself. Pragmatism led him to envision his first film as a kind of coming-of-age reunion picture that could be shot in one location, a story of parted friends who reconvene during a summer weekend in New England. He told *Film Quarterly* in 1981:

> Because I was only writing horror movies and it was going to be three or four years before I was writing more legitimate movies, I wanted to speed up the process. I knew I was going to have about $40,000 together and I wrote a screenplay that we could shoot for that much money. . . . I was going to have non–Screen Actors Guild actors, and all the people I knew that were good, and not in the Guild, were around thirty. So it became a movie about turning thirty, among other things. I knew I wouldn't have enough time for camera movement or a whole lot of action, so there was going to be a lot of people talking, which is what these people I know do on a weekend. . . . It became a reunion in New Hampshire with a bunch of people turning thirty.[5]

The picture unfolds in North Conway, New Hampshire, as schoolteachers Mike and Katie prepare their rented summer home for a reunion of old friends from their days as political activists in the late sixties and early seventies. The two exchange conversation from different rooms, alternately chatting about the sexual proclivities of their visitors while discussing cleaning the toilet and making up beds. This technique of interspersing revealing dialogue with more mundane chat continues throughout the film, as one of the trademark elements of the Sayles style.

The next scene introduces J. T., a would-be singer-songwriter attempting to hitch a ride to Katie and Michael's, battered Gibson guitar by his side. He is spotted and picked up by friend Frances, who happens by on her way to the same destination. Back at home, Katie is still musing about where to put their soon-to-arrive guests while Michael continues his search for a sponge. Meanwhile, Irene and new beau Chip attempt to read a map by a wooded roadside, while they discuss Chip's potential problems of fitting in with the group. Chip's visible unease at the prospect of meeting Irene's friends provides the viewer with an outsider's perspective. Irene is concerned about the impression nervous Chip will make on her friends, and advises him to "act the way you always do, only a little looser."

Michael meets Frances and Chip when he picks up tickets from a local playhouse where another friend, Lacey, is to perform in a "reconstruction comedy." Mike, Katie, Frances, and J. T. are all curious about the newcomer; all they know about him is that he is "a little straight." After fixing a flat tire, Irene and Chip pull into a gas station, where they meet Ron, an attendant and friend of Michael's who has never left the town where they grew up. Ron pumps their gas and teases Chip, adding to the latter's insecurity. Finally they arrive at Michael and Katie's, where Chip momentarily finds himself lost in all of the greetings and hugs the others give one another.

The theme of the outsider and his awkward attempts to be accepted by the group, along with their gradually subsiding unease with him, is one of the important recurring motifs in *Secaucus Seven*. Virtually the only knowledge that Mike, Katie and the others have of Chip is that he works with Irene for a U.S. senator. This kernel of information sparks speculation, as Mike wonders aloud, "He might be forty. . . . We probably should have got some Jim Beam or Johnny Walker." Although Chip is only a year or so older than the rest, he is obviously more self-conscious and less spontaneous than the others, and he is often left out when the others reminisce about past experiences.

Moreover, Chip's sense of timing does not jibe with the others. For example, while some of the others revel in telling flatulence jokes at the breakfast table, Chip is noticeably distracted and disgusted by such banter. The next day, the others are too hungover to have any interest in eating breakfast. Chip wolfs down his eggs, prompting Katie to observe, "You're inhuman." Chip shows his ineptitude at charades, a game the others enjoy, and is too uncoordinated to have any success playing basketball with the men. Even the moniker *Secaucus Seven* that Mike, Katie, Frances, Maura, Jeff, Irene, and J. T. have humorously adopted has its origins in a shared initiation that suggests the group may never completely take another into its fold.

Later, the group gathers in the living room *sans* Jeff and Maura, who are obligated to attend a thirty-fifth wedding anniversary celebration for Jeff's parents. Mike steers the discussion to his travails as a teacher in Boston: "It's mostly discipline. No matter how jazzed up and relevant I try to make the history, I'm still dealing with a roomful of teenage libido." J. T. reveals more of his character as well, affecting the demeanor of a problem student's chiding Mike about his "socialistic tendencies" and telling him to "get bent."

While the friends sunbathe in the garden, Katie muses about Lacey's play that they are planning to attend that night; she dismisses it merely as "free entertainment." The telephone rings, and Katie excuses herself to answer the call. Assuming it to be Ron, Mike launches into a critique of his former high school friend, assailing his immaturity and lack of ambition. Katie returns to say that the caller is not Ron but an upset Maura, waiting at a nearby tourist trap for a ride to join her friends after suddenly severing her relationship with Jeff. Mike and Katie fetch her in their Volkswagen beetle. Back at the lodge, J. T. greets Maura with hugs, to which she responds, "What's a reunion without a little drama?"

Her remark makes for a clever cut to the following scene at the theater, where several of the group discuss Lacey's modest acting abilities. Katie cuts up over Lacey's blurb in the program and the lights go down. The play proves to be an amateurish farce further marred by ludicrous acting; the friends are in consensus, with the approving Chip the exception. The group goes backstage to say hello to Lacey, whose melodramatic gesturing and self-important speeches show her to be a misguided prima donna. She declines Mike's invitation to join them in order to romantically pursue a male member of her troupe. The group leaves the theater in couples, with only Frances walking alone behind the others.

Back at the house, Katie and Mike show Frances, Irene, and Chip a cake decorated with a guitar for J. T.'s birthday. After some discussion, however, they decide against surprising him with it, so as not to depress him at the prospect of turning thirty. Outside, Maura strolls with J. T. and confides to him about her failed relationship with his best friend, Jeff. "All that kept us going was inertia."

After the guests retire, Katie can't sleep for worrying about them. She wonders aloud about conservative Chip, and ponders Irene's many former beaus, which include J. T. and a "loser" named Dwight. Out in the living room, Maura is sleepless as well. She and J. T. share some intimate conversation and soon find themselves having sex together. Meanwhile, Katie's concerns about "everybody breaking up" becomes a philosophical excursion into the viability of relationships in general, and Mike tries to comfort her. She gets up to use the bathroom, but returns immediately when she discovers that "someone is getting it on" in the living room. Katie and Mike think it is Frances who is making love with J. T., but on the living room floor we see a sleepless Frances listening painfully to the amorous couple. Katie returns to the bathroom and runs into Maura coming out—she and Mike revise their original conclusion about who has been making love. When they hear a loud bump overhead from Irene and Chip's room, Mike wonders in mock disbelief, "What did you put in the food?"

Saturday morning, after breakfast, the friends gather for a game of volleyball; on the sidelines, Mike fills Chip in on the histories of the various group members. Meanwhile, Jeff arrives at the town gas station and exchanges a few words with Ron, who invites him for a game of basketball. Jeff arrives unexpectedly at the lodge, interrupting the volleyball game. Later, J. T. confesses to Jeff about his liaison with Maura; Jeff pretends not to care, but looks visibly hurt and angered by this admission. Sitting by a creek, Katie warns Maura not to fall for J. T.; they discuss her failed relationship with Jeff. Meanwhile, Irene and Frances also discuss J. T. and his uncertain career prospects; finally Frances, fond of J. T., admits to being disappointed about his affair with Maura.

The men play a spirited game of basketball at the local schoolyard, and Chip is clearly out of his league. The action accelerates furiously, and one of the few bits of subjective sound editing is apparent in the strange, rhythmic heavy breathing noise that accelerates with the pace of the players. The action heats up in a series of camera angles and close handheld camerawork, culminating when Jeff blocks J. T., sending him head first into the basket pole.

Howie, Ron, and Mike repair to a shady wooded spot to rest. Carol catches up with them and tells Howie he has to work at the local ski lodge that night. They talk briefly about his family, ending with Howie's admonition about the decision to have children: "Think long and hard about it, think long and hard." At the house, the women also discuss the ramifications of having children while playing a game of Clue; their opinions mostly reflect ambivalence.

At a nearby creek, the men dive naked into the chilly water while the women watch from some rocks. Katie marvels with amusement at Chip's ample endowments while Irene teases Frances about Ron's apparent interest in her. Between dunks, Chip and Jeff argue politics while J. T. confides to Mike that he is broke. Later, Ron rhapsodizes to Frances about snowmobiles in the woods. Mike is incredulous when Jeff, a drug counselor, accidentally drops a small bindle of heroin given to him by one of his wards at the rehabilitation clinic.

A short montage illustrates the idiosyncrasies of each individual as they prepare food for a barbecue: an intense Jeff slaps hamburger into patties, Katy gleefully pours multiple cups of wine, while Chip bumbles through the simple chore of shelling hard-boiled eggs. Irene conducts a mock interview with Chip, who shows a rare sense of humor as a glib politico circumlocuting about a tomato. The conversation turns to marijuana and

Chip announces that he has brought some "dynamite stuff" along with him in the glove compartment of his car.

That evening after ostensibly smoking some of the herb, Mike, Maura, J. T., Jeff, Katie, Irene, Chip, and Frances meet Ron and Howie at a local tavern, and partake in a variety of conversations and activities. A young woman with a sweet candy voice plays guitar and sings a blues song, J. T. and Frances thumbwrestle, Katie orders a bottle of light beer, and Chip and Jeff have a heated political discussion as the crowd drowns them out. One of the film's few dolly shots follows Katie as she carries the beers back to her table; Howie, Ron, and Mike reminisce about high school friends. J. T. and Jeff strike up some conversation with two women, but Jeff backs off and they leave to go to the lady's room. Ron, Mike, and Howie do an amusing take on an auto racing commercial until Howie is paged by his wife. Chip sings a folk ditty with two others, following solo with a song of his own about a young loser who doesn't know what to do with himself.

In a secluded corner, Ron and Frances chat with one another about their chosen work. He asks if she wants to thumbwrestle, and when she declines, he suggests they "tonguewrestle" instead. He asks if she wants to get a room at the lodge. Katie works up to more potent drinks, but when Chip tries to order a beer, the bartender asks for identification. A sudden outburst silences the crowd as Jeff and Maura shout at one another, effectively bringing an end to the group's evening festivities. They argue heatedly, displaying to all their basic incompatibilities and lack of communication.

Brash Ron and sheepish Frances appear at Howie's lodge to book a room for the night. The others, however, have squeezed into Chip's car for the journey back. They stop to investigate something blocking the road: a deer, dead and bound, has been left after apparently falling off another car. Police appear and detain the group for questioning at the local jail for illegally killing a deer, a charge Jeff refers to as "Bambicide." Jeff, in particular, takes great relish in describing his various arrests for activism, all charges for which had been dropped. When Maura is quizzed and her answers match Jeff's identically ("Same as his" is her answer to nearly every question), she realizes how much her life has intertwined with Jeff's. Mike and J. T. tease a worried Chip about the arrest until they realize that his car contains marijuana. The friends reminisce and relate the story of how they became the "Secaucus Seven." Mike tells Chip how Katie, Jeff, Maura, Frances, Irene, and J. T. were stopped en route to a Washington march and arrested when their borrowed car was found to contain "a rifle and an ounce of dope." He explains that the charges were dropped and the seven were released after spending a night in jail. After a local drunk confesses to the crime and they are released, Mike reels when he finds out that Jeff has been holding the heroin the whole time in his shirt pocket.

Returning from their brush with the law, some of the group attempt to resolve misgivings about their relationships with one another. Chip is crestfallen when Irene tells him that Ron is one of the many men she has slept with, but seems willing to put his feelings aside as he responds to her invitation to make love. Jeff admits to J. T. that he is angry over his best friend's sleeping with his former love, but advises him not to "lose any sleep over it."

The next day only Chip eats the scrambled eggs Mike has cooked, as the others nurse hangovers from the previous evening's festivities. When Frances arrives from her night out with Ron, the group serenades her in unison: "Hey there, you with the stars in your eyes." Outside, a concerned Irene offers J. T. a loan of two thousand dollars, which he graciously refuses. All gather in front of the house to bid Chip and Irene farewell. Shortly thereafter, an agitated Jeff chops wood alone in the backyard; he disappears without saying goodbye, leaving behind only a pile of kindling and an apologetic note. While Frances sleeps on the sofa, a weary Mike considers taking down the volleyball net before it rains. The film ends with a medium closeup of Katie, who muses wistfully, "What are we going to do with all those eggs?"

The early 1980s saw a youth zeitgeist that, unlike the collective spirit of the late 1960s, was fragmented and wracked with pessimism, characterized by former Sex Pistols' singer Johnny Rotten's rant "No future" than by former Beatle John Lennon's chant of "Power to the people." It would take the unfortunate event of Lennon's assassination by a demented fan in December 1980 to bring America's youth together again in sixties fashion, but before that, in the spring of the year, there was John Sayles's *The Return of the Secaucus Seven* to reunite a group of former sixties activists and remind them how much had changed in the decade since the Woodstock generation celebrated three days of music, peace, and love.

Secaucus Seven was among the first of films to deal with survivors of the "sixties generation" contemplating how best to navigate the brave new world of the Reagan years after the "me decade" of the seventies. These former were not among the newly dubbed "yuppies," who were interested in "having it all now." Frances, for example, who has chosen a potentially lucrative professional career path as a doctor, is disturbed and disillusioned with her crass and cynical mentors. Others, most notably Jeff, are suspicious of the prevailing sociopolitical system in general.

Among the many issues addressed in *The Return of the Secaucus Seven*, perhaps the most important is the nature of community and the individual's place in it. Another key concern of the characters is the reconciliation of their youthful ideals with the realities and limitations of career options open to them. Many of them have a history of socially responsible activism, but they seem plagued with ambivalence and contradictory inclinations. We learn that Mike, Jeff, and Maura have all served in Vista, the now-defunct domestic equivalent of the Peace Corps. While some of them have been successful pursuing socially redeeming work, as in the teaching careers of Mike and Katie, others have been less successful. Maura, for one, has abandoned acting but seems to be searching for some kind of meaningful career as well as a fulfilling relationship, which she has not realized with Jeff. And Jeff, while employed in the most socially committed occupation of the group as a drug counselor, openly admits to enjoying "getting stoned" and seems to want to try the heroin he carries throughout the film.

Some of the other characters have had to learn the game of compromise in order to further their ideological goals. Irene professes not to "give a rat's ass about the senator" for whom she works, but does so as an "infiltrator," using her job as a "form of subversion" to help "people in state agencies . . . doing good stuff like housing and drug education," people who likely would be out of a job if a less liberal official were elected. Frances, a medical student and the most successful member in traditional terms, clearly despises her mentors at the hospital where she interns (at one point referring to the doctors as "douche bags"), but seems profoundly committed to the joys and responsibilities of becoming an obstetrician.

The question of raising children arises throughout the film. While playing a game of Clue, the women acknowledge that they are passing through their prime childbearing years but cannot decide whether—or more important, with whom—to raise children. Only a minor character, Howie, has any children, and he complains about the responsibilities and the loss of freedom that has come with family life. But there are rewards in child raising as well, as he beams proudly to Mike and Ron about his son and daughters in a rare moment of reflection in the local tavern.

The most frustrated of the characters, Katie, is perhaps the most human in many ways. She certainly has the sharpest tongue of the characters. But she also expresses the most concern over the inevitable unraveling of the group. Worrying about where to put her overnight guests, Katie quips that because she and Mike are shouldering the burden of hosting the reunion, "people ought to just strike up a relationship with whoever we put 'em in with." In reality, however, she frets about the ephemeral nature of her friends' couplings and worries about the future of her own relationship with Mike. Her insecurity manifests itself in snide comments about other women whom Mike has associated with, most notably thespian Lacey, whom Katie mercilessly disparages.

The simplest and perhaps most sincere character is the outsider Chip, who alone has made it past thirty with his naïveté intact; Irene quips that he cries even when hearing the Gettysburg Address. This attribute makes him the butt of the others' teasing, as when Jeff verbally pummels him about his senator. Other events distance him from the others as well: his social awkwardness, his ineptitude at games, his uncritical praise of Lacey's play, his morning-after voracity. But Chip is the sole member of the group to undergo any change during the course of the film, realizing a newfound ease on his departure; he tells Irene, "I think I passed the test." Interestingly, it is Chip's simplistic idealism that wins him the acceptance of the group. Unlike the others, however, self-examination has made him more comfortable with himself.

J. T., the most spontaneous and charming (as well as the least introspective) of the group, is also the most irresponsible and least likely to succeed. His aspirations to make it as a singer-songwriter are unfocused and unrealistic at best. His songs, all about naïve young losers oddly reminiscent of himself, are neither masterful nor memorable. Of all the "Secaucus Seven," however, he is the one who still holds the yearnings and hopes of having an uncompromised career—one the others have reluctantly adjusted or at least questioned. He admits to having no money, but when Irene offers him an "investment in his career" of two thousand dollars, he turns it down in an admirable and disarming display of candor. In a particularly moving scene, he explains his wanting to succeed or fail without any help from others, lest he become one of the "professional drinking companions" he sees often in bars, who are supported by their old friends "who keep them around to remind them of what it was like to be young and irresponsible."

Secaucus Seven is one of the few independent films to eschew overt visual style in favor of writing and character development. Perhaps because he did not attend a film school, Sayles stands alone among independents in his refusal to litter his films with allusory homages to other films, a predilection shared by countless film school alumni ranging from Brian DePalma to Spike Lee. As Sayles once told an interviewer, "I want people to leave the theater thinking about their own lives, not about other movies."[6]

The visual look of the film has been likened to that of a home movie, owing in large degree to the grainy 16mm format. Sayles has also admitted that the straightforward unadorned visuals, if not intentional, were a natural consequence of the extreme low budget with which he had to work. Most of the shots *are* fairly tight to deemphasize any background elements. To be sure, there are also awkward dissolves that appear to exist more to patch continuity breaks than to fulfill any aesthetic purpose. But it is this very lack of style that gives it authenticity. The self-conscious, arty style of *Eraserhead* or *Stranger Than Paradise* would have been completely misplaced here. Despite the film's seeming artlessness, at least one visual reference to a work of fine art can be viewed in the skinny-dipping scene, as Ron and Chip assume sculptural poses to show off their musculature in a pastiche of a painting by nineteenth-century American painter Thomas Eakins. Interestingly, *Secaucus Seven* established Sayles as a director less interested in visual style than in storytelling nuance, a notion later belied by such visually lyrical films as *Matewan* and *The Secret of Roan Inish*.

When asked if he placed *Secaucus Seven* into any particular genre, Sayles replied: "The American equivalent of that is the movies they made during World War II about a bunch of guys going through basic training and then into the army. It really wasn't about one individual."[7] A more obvious antecedent might be the European "weekend in the country" social critiques epitomized by such films as *Rules of the Game* and *Smiles of a Summer Night*. But whereas Renoir and Bergman used film as a vehicle to criticize the amorality and decadence of the upper middle class, Sayles turns a much more sympathetic ear to his working-class and lower-middle-class characters. Even this gathering would not be complete, however, without the requisite sexual dalliances to stir passions and jealousies. Indeed, one of the most interesting features of the film is the ease with which it treats issues of promiscuity and casual sex—it is difficult to imagine such free rein of the senses occurring in the safe-sex nineties. *Secaucus Seven* was released when the sexual revolution was in full swing, two years before medical science would "discover" AIDS and six years before actor Rock Hudson's death would forever change the way most Americans regard casual sexual relations.

Critics generally lauded *Secaucus Seven* for its writing and ensemble work. Those who found fault were put off by the sometimes awkward acting, its often workmanlike editing, the unaesthetic visuals, and general lack of production values. David Sterrit wrote that the film was "a fictionalized home movie, nothing more . . . " and advised his readers to "never trust a picture that opens with a closeup of a plunger." But even while Andrew Sarris observed that "the people looked awkwardly real . . . and the *mise-en-scene* seemed to lack the deep planes of visual complexity," he still gave the film a favorable review.

Sayles developed a number of projects after *Secaucus Seven*, including scripts for *The Howling* and *The Clan of the Cave Bear*, a TV series entitled *Shannon's Deal*, and a major novel, *Los Gusanos* (The Worms). He was aided in his work by his award of a John D. and Catherine T. MacArthur "genius" grant in 1983, which paid him $30,000 annually for five years. He also wrote and directed two one-act plays, *New Hope for the Dead* and *Turnbuckle*, which opened to disappointing critical notices.

His most interesting serious work, however, has continued to be his own films, which he has produced mostly outside the constraints of the Hollywood system. His next film after *Secaucus Seven* was another low-budget independent feature, *Lianna* (1983), which portrayed a young woman who leaves her children and philandering husband to live with her lesbian lover and mentor. After her lover leaves her for a job in another town, she ventures bravely to seek companionship in gay bars, risking ostracism among her peers in the small town where she lives. The picture is remarkable for its unflinching look at male pride and sexism, its refusal to trade in stereotypes and voyeurism regarding heterosexual and lesbian sexual relationships and dating ritual, and the remarkable absence of heavy-handed moralizing regarding sex roles and choices.

Sayles also made his first studio-financed film, *Baby It's You*, in 1983. This unsentimental revisitation of the Romeo-and-Juliet theme was easily one of Sayles's most commercially successful films, perhaps because of the familiar elements of its storyline and high school setting.

In 1984, Sayles unveiled his quirkiest offering to date, *The Brother from Another Planet*. A witty and gently satirical rejoinder to the movie *ET* and its ilk, *Brother* examined themes of racism with a black humanoid who flees slavery on a distant planet to seek sanctuary on earth, in Harlem. Sayles's wit and light touch continued to subvert expectations in *Brother*, with unique characters, discursive, elliptical exchanges of dialogue, and a thoughtful exploration of Harlem's contemporary social mores substituting for the usual one-dimensional characters and special-effects displays integral to most films of the "alien from outer space" genre.

Matewan, perhaps Sayles's most socially committed film, was released in 1987, garnering lukewarm audience response. An involving, heartfelt chronicle of a coal miners' strike and subsequent struggle with mining company strikebreakers in the titular West Virginia town, *Matewan* used the genre of the western to temper myth with unvarnished realism, examining the chasm between individualism and collective action in its grim and gritty portrayal of simple people caught in an inexorable chain of events. Given the movie-going public's indifference to westerns and political-theme films, or perhaps its inability to follow a story inhabited by numerous well-developed characters, the film languished and indeed failed to break even at the box office.

Sayles got his opportunity to direct a project he had entertained from his earliest days as a screenwriter with the film *Eight Men Out* (1988). An account of the infamous "Black Sox" scandal of 1919, *Eight Men Out* pitted the hapless players of Chicago's White Sox against ruthless and exploitative ball club owners.

Less-than-ideal experiences with Hollywood on the films *Baby It's You* and *Eight Men Out* prompted Sayles to seek independent financing for his next ventures, *City of Hope*, a multicharacter study of urban longing and despair, and *Passion Fish*, an Oscar-nominated story of a woman who returns to her Louisiana home after suffering a paralyzing accident.

Sayles completed *The Secret of Roan Inish* in 1994. *The New York Times'* Steven Holden wrote about Sayles's most recent venture:

> Examining the obscure Celtic legend of the Selkie, a creature who is half human and half seal, he has created a touching cinematic meditation on people, familial roots and the myths that sustain them.[8]

In the years following *The Return of the Secaucus Seven*, other films and television programs, most notably Lawrence Kasdan's *The Big Chill* and

Edward Zwick's television series *thirtysomething*, would revisit many of the same themes, but few could capture the unassuming wit, authenticity and resonance of Sayles's seminal motion picture. When asked to comment on the suspicious similarity between *Secaucus Seven* and *Chill*, Sayles graciously replied:

> It's a different movie. It's called *The Big Chill* for a reason. It's a film about people who have either lost their ideals or are realizing they never had them in the first place. *Secaucus Seven* is about people who are desperately, desperately trying to hold onto their ideals. That's a very different group. *Chill* people are more upper-middle class. The *Secaucus* group is more lower-middle class; some of them are probably the first people in their families who went to a four-year college. And they've chosen to be downwardly mobile.[9]

It is fitting that Sayles himself has eschewed upward mobility in the film industry, determined to dictate his own terms as a filmmaker who still holds ideals others have long abandoned. In so doing, he has become a paradigm of the committed filmmaker.

NOTES

1. Kent Black, "A Man and His Myth," *Los Angeles Times*, February 5, 1995, p. E5.

2. He once proudly pointed out to an interviewer that he "came from a working-class family and went to a working-class high school in a working-class city"; see Black, "A Man and His Myth," p. E5.

3. John Sayles, interview. David Chute, "Designated Writer: An Interview with John Sayles," *Film Comment*, May-June 1981, p. 57.

4. Ibid., p. 57.

5. John Sayles, interview. T. Schlesinger, "Putting People Together: An Interview with John Sayles," *Film Quarterly*, Summer 1981, p. 6.

6. Ibid., p. 7.

7. Ibid., p. 6.

8. Stephen Holden, "The Secret of Roan Inish," *New York Times*, v. 144, col. 1, February 3, 1995, p. B3(N) p. C12(L).

9. John Sayles, interview. Claudia Dreyfus, *The Progressive*, November 1991, p. 32.

CHAPTER 3

Koan-undrum:
Chan Is Missing
(1981)

USA: Unrated

16mm Black and White

Running time: 80 minutes

Directed by Wayne Wang

Cast in alphabetical order:

Frankie Alarcon. . . . . Frankie

Virginia Cerenio. . . . . Jenny's Friend

Roy Chan. . . . . Mr. Lee

Laureen Chew. . . . . Amy

Marc Hayashi. . . . . Steve

Wood Moy. . . . . Jo

Judi Nihei. . . . . Lawyer

Presco Tabios. . . . . Presco

Peter Wang. . . . . Henry the Cook

George Woo. . . . . George

Emily Yamasaki. . . . . Chan's Daughter

Ellen Yeung. . . . . Mrs. Chan Hung

Cinematography by Michael G. Chin

Music by Robert Kikuchi-Yngojo

Edited by Wayne Wang

Produced by Wayne Wang

> The audience I wanted to reach was the Asian-Americans of my generation . . . The only aspect I thought about for the American audience was the aesthetics, the more formal aspect: the structure of the film, how it was shot, and taking a *film noir* and reworking it.
>
> Wayne Wang[1]

A most unlikely film noir–cinema verité hybrid, billed as the first American feature film made by an all Asian-American cast and crew, *Chan Is Missing* appeared on the festival circuit in 1982 and met with almost unanimous critical approval. Long before the critical triumphs of shoestring productions such as *El Mariachi* and *Slacker*, *Chan Is Missing* became one of the first "no-budget" films to grace many of the year's ten-best lists of major critics. Considered by some to be the sleeper of 1982, *Chan Is Missing* was the first of director Wayne Wang's films to examine his own mixed and often contradictory feelings about his Chinese-American heritage.

Ostensibly a detective movie, *Chan Is Missing* actually functions more as a thoughtful and amusing study of two cultures in collision: Chinese immigrants and Chinese-Americans wrestle with American culture while struggling to retain their Chinese identity and rich traditional heritage. Set in San Francisco's Chinatown, the film centers on the efforts of a middle-aged Chinese-American cabbie and his young nephew to track down a mysterious acquaintance who has disappeared with $4,000 of their savings in a scheme purported to get them a taxi license.

Wang (whose given name derives from American actor John Wayne) was born in 1949, six days after his parents arrived in Hong Kong as refugees from mainland China. Wang remembers growing up on a steady diet of American B-movies, notably Audie Murphy films, and he cultivated a special appreciation for the films of Frank Capra as well as Japanese director Ozu.

After emigrating to the United States, Wang attended Foothill College, then studied painting at California College of Arts and Crafts (affiliated at the time with the San Francisco Art Institute). He gravitated toward film-making and photography, and graduated in 1972 with a master of fine arts degree. His first feature film, entitled *A Man, a Woman, and a Killer*, was made in 1972 as a $16,000 collaborative effort with fellow independent Rick Schmidt. As with several other American independent productions, the film fared well at European festivals but was ignored by American critics; aside from a three-day stint at New York's Bleecker Street Cinema, it never found domestic distribution. Wang made several more short films before returning to Hong Kong in hopes of breaking into the Hong Kong entertainment industry. He worked as assistant director for Chinese sequences in the film *Golden Needles* and was hired as director of a "straightforward *All in the Family* kind of soap opera" entitled *Below the Lion Rock*.[2]

Negative experiences on these productions sent Wang back to the United States. Back in California, Wang worked for public television in the Bay Area and temporarily abandoned filmmaking to do community service work in the Chinatown district of San Francisco. His immersion in the problems experienced by Chinese immigrants became the impetus for *Chan Is Missing*, as he later explained:

> *Chan Is Missing* was shot after I had been in Hong Kong and was feeling guilty about the fact that I could no longer fit in my own culture. So when I came back to the United States, I submerged myself in Chinatown and went overboard in becoming Chinese. And that was the point when I realized that the Chinese and American worlds don't necessarily blend that well together. You sort of bounce back and forth between the two. And coming to terms with that and expressing that collision of cultures inside myself were the emotional reasons for the birth of *Chan Is Missing*.[3]

Wang conceived the film as a thirty-minute documentary about taxi cab drivers, but he began developing it as a feature after receiving grant monies from the American Film Institute. "After I got the initial amount," he told Richard Patterson, "I was crazy enough to say 'I'm gonna do a feature.' I figured that I might be able to shoot the whole film on that budget and get it into the lab—for $7,875 (the total of the first two installments of the grant)."[4] Wang earned money for the venture by writing science courses for children. The script evolved into a fictional mystery that revolved around two characters and relied heavily on nonsynchronous dialogue sequences. Virtually all of the characters and extras who appeared in the film are of Asian lineage. Wang guessed that he could shoot the film in ten weekends of one-half day each for forty scenes.

Chan Is Missing premiered at Berkeley's Pacific Film Archive, followed by screenings at the Roxy Theater in San Francisco, but Wang had little success in finding a distributor. The film went relatively unnoticed until it appeared at the 1982 FILMEX and the Museum of Modern Art's New Directors/New Films series, where it met with positive reviews. New Yorker Films agreed to distribute *Chan Is Missing* and put up the money for a 35mm blowup and music rights. The film became a surprise hit and grossed over $1 million, more than fifty times its production budget.

The film opens as Jo, a pudgy and unassuming middle-aged Chinese-American cab driver and an unlikely protagonist by any stretch, drives his cab through the streets of Chinatown. The passing scenery creates beautiful moving reflections that obscure Jo's face in one of many visually ambiguous shots in the film. This scene demonstrates many of the techniques that form the style of this picture—grainy cinema verité style black-and-white photography, seedy—though not menacing—scenes of street life, POV hand-held camera. Jo voices his irreverent and witty thoughts in an interior monologue that recalls the classic hard-boiled investigator formula:

> **JO (VOICEOVER):** There's a game I play, one thousand, two thousand, three thousand . . .
>
> **FARE (OFFSCREEN):** Hey, what's a good place to eat in Chinatown?
>
> **JO (VOICEOVER):** Under three seconds, that question comes up under three seconds ninety percent of the time. I usually give them my routine on the differences between Mandarin and Cantonese food and get a *good* tip.

Steve, Jo's brash young nephew, is eating Chinese takeout with Jo's niece Amy in the kitchen when Jo arrives home. Steve jokes about eating at home rather than patroning a restaurant that caters to Communist Chinese sympathizers. They banter about many subjects, including a flag-waving incident at a parade. In a voiceover, Jo explains:

> My nephew Steve and I decided to get a cab license so we can be our own boss. We had to sublease the license from an independent owner in Chinatown. My niece Amy and my friend Chan Hung helped set up the deal. The thing was that Chan Hung had to take cash to go finalize everything. Steve felt uneasy about that, but Amy and I convinced him that that would be OK. But I'm a little worried about Chan Hung—Steve and I haven't seen him in a few days.

Jo and Steve meet at a local cafe for breakfast the next week. A loquacious woman looking for Chan interrupts them, explaining that for a class she is writing a paper on "The Legal Implications of Cross-Cultural Misunderstanding." She wants to interview Chan about an automobile accident he had the previous week. Steve barely conceals his boredom at her long-winded explanation when she reveals that Chan did not appear at his court hearing. Her rambling dissertation is the first of many lessons the pair receive about the dichotomy of East-West thinking and its ramifications for the Chinese-American community; her discourse, however, interests them more for its modest clue. Following the lead, Jo and Steve seek out Chan at his apartment but find no one home.

Steve nonchalantly cracks a Chinese-American joke over beers with Jo, reminding the older cabbie of a cook at the Golden Dragon restaurant. In a flashback, the cook, Henry, wears a "Samurai Night Fever" T-shirt, guzzles (and appears not to enjoy) glasses of milk, chain-smokes, and croons "Fry me to the moon." While at work at the bustling Golden Dragon, Henry rambles on about a number of subjects in English and Chinese, none of them shedding any light on Chan's disappearance. Thus, the pair is led down the first of many blind alleys in their search for the missing Chan.

A long sequence shot leads Jo and Steve down a Chinatown sidewalk in a casual exchange; Steve chides Jo that his recent divorce from his "F.O.B." ("fresh off the boat") is coloring his judgement in the Chan disappearance— an allegation Jo shrugs off. At home, Jo receives his next lead in the form of a telephone answering machine message from Steve: Chan spent a good deal of time working at a Manilatown senior center. An inquiry at the center turns up Chan's coat, which contains a number of documents in the pockets: a package of crackers, a will written in Chinese, and a newspaper clipping. The center manager relates some news about Chan's apparent intentions to go to mainland China. A Filipino employee tells Jo and Steve a cryptic anecdote instructing them to "look in the puddle" that yields a reflection of oneself.

Jo and Steve take turns staking out the St. Paul Hotel, where Chan has kept a room. Impatient, they return to knock at the door; again, no one answers. A voice from the room across the hall tells them that a "woman in red" took some pictures from Chan Hung, and teases them with "just the facts, Ma'am" *Dragnet* references and other amusing taunts. The owner of the voice refuses to reveal himself, and the two go away empty-handed.

That night, Jo revisits the room with a passkey borrowed from the hotel manager. Inside he finds nothing but three sketchy clues: a newspaper with an article about the "flag-waving incident," a newspaper front page from which a news item has been ripped, and four loops of masking tape on the wall marking the spot where a picture was mounted. In voiceover, Jo reveals that the date of the torn newspaper page matches the date of the article found in Chan's jacket. He goes on to describe his attempts to interview an old man implicated in a shooting that occurred in a heated political disagreement after the parade incident. The man, who has been released on bail, refuses to speak to Jo, telling him only to "look for the woman."

Another phone message from Steve reveals that a woman had turned up at the taxi garage looking for Chan, and that Steve followed her home. "Maybe she's the woman everyone's talking about," Jo muses. Jo and Steve find the woman, who turns out to be Chan's estranged wife, and her daughter at their brownstone. Mrs. Chan apologizes that she is pressed for time, but tells some things about Chan that are amusingly drowned out from some loud Chinese rock music blasting from the next room. Nonetheless, her most revealing observation is that Chan "was too Chinese" to successfully assimilate into American culture, and admits that she and Chan have been separated for over a year.

Out on the street, Steve mimics Latino and black street jargon while reading aloud to Jo from a newspaper. Doggedly searching for any lead that might help him solve the mystery of Chan's disappearance, Jo visits George at the Newcomers Language Center. George affirms that Chan was indeed having difficulties fitting in. Unfortunately, Jo finds no substantive leads there, and is instead subjected to more diatribes on Chinese-American relations. George points to a boxed pie from a Chinese bakery as a metaphor for Chinese-American assimilation:

> The way we need to deal with it is to be Chinese-American—to take the good things from our background and also try to take the good things from this country to try to enhance our life. Sun Wah Kue's apple pie: it is a definite American form—pie—and it looks like any other apple pie, but it doesn't taste like any other apple pie . . . and that's because many Chinese baking techniques have gone into it. When we deal with it in our everyday life, that's what we have to do.

Jo leaves disappointed but amused about George's take on Chinese-American politics. On the street Steve and Jo have a chance encounter with Chan's daughter Jenny and a friend. Jenny reaffirms what the others have told them about Chan's reluctance to assimilate, and reveals the name and whereabouts of Chan's sponsor, Mr. Lee. Jo meets with Mr. Lee, who hasn't seen Chan since he was involved in a minor automobile accident. Lee is interrupted by a phone call, wherein Lee advises the caller on some finer points of the art of negotiation. Off the phone, he relates an anecdote of another Chinese man's misunderstanding in an auto accident, and tells Joe that Chan was the brains behind the first word-processing system in Chinese.

Jo becomes confused when he sees a community newspaper with a newly published photo of the flag-waving incident, which some say depicted a different event entirely. Jo putters in his kitchen, continuing in his dryly humorous trademark monologue:

> I went home to get a bite to eat. There was only a piece of leftover pizza. Chan Hung used to always talk about how Marco Polo stole everything from us—first pasta, then pizza. Too bad the

Chinese didn't have tomatoes. But I shouldn't complain; the only thing I use my oven for is to store gadgets. I'm no gourmet Chinese cook and I'm no Charlie Chan either, although I did start watching some of his reruns for cheap laughs. Charlie says, 'When superior man have no clue, be patient; maybe he become lucky.' "

The next night Jo cleans out the cab Chan drove before he disappeared, finding a letter written in Chinese and addressed to Chan and a pistol under the front seat.

George translates the letter for Jo; it appears to be from Chan's brother, advising Chan to be careful about "people from the left" who might be "after him."

Jo relates that police are still seeking the gun in the flag-waving incident and Steve tells Jo he thinks that Chan was the shooter in the flag-waving incident aftermath, but the old man charged with the crime denied that assertion.

Jo goes to the old address and hears from a neighbor that Chan hasn't lived there for six months. A woman telephones Jo, telling him to stop asking questions about Chan. Jo is in a quandary and muses, "Maybe Chan Hung really did kill that guy [the neighbor] instead of the old man [who has been charged with the crime]. Maybe if I know all this and someone knows I know it, maybe they don't want me to know."

A montage finds Jo wandering paranoid among street sights while some frenzied mystery music plays on the track. Many of the images are minimal: a POV through the windshield of a moving automobile, signs, passersby.

In one of the film's key sequences, a handheld camera underlines the tension of a conversation Jo and Steve have along the waterfront. Steve insists they report Chan's disappearance and apparent theft to the police, but Jo refuses. Steve doesn't understand Jo's sympathy for Chan Hung's plight. After sharing beers in stony silence, the two look up Jenny Chan at a local restaurant. She emerges from the back of the restaurant and joins them at a table and hands Steve an envelope. Upon opening it, Steve sees that it contains their $4,000. Jenny conveys Chan's apologies for failing to secure the taxi license, but claims ignorance of her father's whereabouts.

On a city street, Jo has a conversation in Chinese with a man dressed in coat and tie, Mr. Fong. No subtitles clarify this conversation, but Jo's voiceover afterward admits that "Mr. Fong didn't come up with the important clue. He told me that to solve the mystery, I had to think Chinese."

In a cab parked beneath the Golden Gate Bridge, Jo tells Steve a Chinese riddle told to him by Mr. Fong. The riddle, a variant on the "lady and the tiger" theme, concerns a farmer who can't pay his rent. His landlord issues an ultimatum: settle the debt or send his daughter to him. The landlord provides a way out for the girl, offering her a choice between two doors:

one leads outside, the other to his bedroom. Of course, the daughter understands the ruse—that both doors in fact lead to the bedroom. She points to one of the doors, saying "that is not the one that leads outside." Jo concludes, "She was trying to use the negative to emphasize the positive."

Over a closeup shot of rippling water, Jo thinks aloud:

> This mystery is appropriately Chinese: what's not there seems to have just as much meaning as what is there. The murder article's not there, the photograph's not there, the other woman's not there, Chan Hung's not there, nothing is what it seems to be. I guess I'm not Chinese enough. I can't accept a mystery without a solution.

A series of shots of different people waiting at the same bus stop follows, accompanied by a rambling piano score. The rippling water reappears; Jo muses:

> I've already given up on finding out what happened to Chan Hung. But what bothers me is that I no longer know who Chan Hung really is. Mr. Lee says Chan Hung and immigrants like him need to be taught everything as if they were children. Mr. Fong thinks anyone who can invent a word processing system in Chinese must be a genius, Steve thinks that Chan Hung is slow-witted but sly when it comes to money. Jenny thinks her father is honest and trustworthy. Mrs. Chan thinks her husband is a failure because he isn't rich. Amy thinks he is a hotheaded political activist. The old man thinks Chan Hung's just a paranoid person. Henry thinks Chan Hung is patriotic and has gone back to the mainland to serve the people. Frankie thinks that Chan Hung worries a lot about money and his inheritance—he thinks that Chan Hung's back in Taiwan, fighting with his brother over the partition of some property. George thinks Chan Hung's too Chinese, and unwilling to change. Presco thinks he's an eccentric who likes Mariachi music.

Jo is once more driving in his cab, reflections spilling across the windshield:

> The problem with me is that I believe what I see and hear. If I did that with Chan Hung I'll know nothing, because everything is so contradictory. Here's a picture of Chan Hung—and I still can't see him.

A Polaroid shows Jo standing in the sunlight alongside a figure underneath an awning, whose head and shoulders are completely obscured in shadow.

The film ends with a scratchy rendition of "Grant Avenue" from Rodgers and Hammerstein's *Flower Drum Song*, which accompanies a montage of Chinese signs and tawdry storefronts, drab buildings, turtles struggling to free themselves from a meat store tank followed by a shot of dead turtles stacked in a cage, an elderly woman rocking aimlessly on a balcony, steaming buckets in a restaurant, posters on a bakery window advertising a "samurai" film, an Italian market topped by a sign hawking "Chop Suey," window photos of Chinese food dishes, old people craning their necks for a bus, a Buddha strung with Christmas tinsel, and laundry hanging from a second-story window.

Chan Is Missing is built upon a series of seemingly irreconcilable dichotomies. First, there are the generational differences between the two protagonists: Steve is young, impatient, and stubborn—he wants only to recover his missing money and fails to see why Jo sympathizes with Chan. Steve continually asserts his wishes to go to the police rather than continue to unravel the mystery on their own. Jo, on the other hand, is thoughtful and inquisitive. He patiently investigates all possible avenues of inquiry, refusing to give up even when his clues lead nowhere.

There is a cultural gap between the pair as well. Jo straddles his Chinese and American heritages somewhat uncomfortably while Steve is thoroughly assimilated into American culture and pokes irreverent fun at Chinese traditions. Steve "jive talks" and frequently undercuts Jo's philosophical and humanistic musings with vulgarities and throwaway jokes. When Jo relates the riddle of the girl who must choose between doors, smirking Steve cracks that "she wants it bad." He teasingly refers to themselves as "Charlie Chan and his number one son," to Jo's visible discomfort. And Steve cannot fathom Jo's consuming interest in Chinese-American tribulations while attempting to solve the mystery.

These dichotomies follow the ancient Chinese philosophical and religious principles of yin and yang—one negative, dark, and feminine (yin); the other positive, bright, and masculine (yang)—whose interaction influences the destinies of all creatures and things. The mystery of the film can be addressed only when Jo approaches his problems along the lines of a Chinese riddle in which unspoken words and unknown facts point toward a solution. The film's story turns as much upon what is not shown (yin) as what is (yang). To Jo, the mystery is more about finding out just who Chan Is than in finding out what he has done with their money. The answer, based on contradictory accounts given by each of the film's characters, is no answer at all but is itself is a riddle. It recalls the story of five blind men who all identify an elephant in entirely different ways, based on which part of the elephant each touches. Jo has but one photo of Chan Hung, but his face is completely shrouded in black shadow. This image recalls a scene from Michelangelo Antonioni's *Blowup,* where the protagonist photographer is left with a single piece of evidence indicating a murder: a grainy and hopelessly indecipherable image of a corpse.

The visual veneer of *Chan Is Missing* 's technique is as deceptive as its subject. Superficially, it resembles a cinema verité documentary in the tradition of the Maysles brothers' *Salesman* or Frederick Wiseman's *Titticut Follies.* Several of the scenes are marred by mismatched lighting, camera fogging, and light flares. Some of the handheld shots seem tentative and inappropriate, while the many jump cuts do not capture the jarring verve of Godard's *Breathless*—by contrast they seem choppy, amateurish. These flaws do not hurt the impact of the film; indeed, they add to its veracity and subtlety.

The considerable irony in the choice of music for *Chan Is Missing* recalls the films of Stanley Kubrick. As the film begins, a familiar song plays, yet the words are strange, indecipherable: it is a Chinese-language interpretation of "Rock Around the Clock." A Chinese rock band sings a cookie-cutter tune that sounds like any one of the many popular corporate rock bands of the day—Foreigner, Journey, or Thin Lizzy—with a Cantonese lead vocal. At the film's close, grim and grimy monochrome images of Chinatown accompany the jaunty strains of "Grant Street, San Francisco" from Rodgers and Hammerstein's *Flower Drum Song.*

The process of watching the film can be likened to meditating on a Zen koan—the point being not to solve the mystery but to gain illumination by forcing one's mind through a paradoxical exercise. As such, the film is not a suspense thriller in the Hitchcock tradition, but an unsolved mystery in the Antonioni and Altman mode. The film pokes fun at the Hitchcock technique of drowning out an important verbal clue with intrusive ambient noise (à la *North by Northwest*), when loud Chinese rock music drowns out a potentially revealing conversation between Jo and Mrs. Chan. *Chan Is Missing* also self-reflexively mocks its own detective film conventions in the same way that Altman's *The Long Goodbye* took aim at the arbitrary rules of the hard-boiled genre it satirized. In *Goodbye,* Elliot Gould's shambling Marlowe tells his interrogators, "This is where I ask 'what's this about?' and you say 'we ask the questions.' " Jo, too, is aware of the familiar detective ritual he is retracing, noting after his and Steve's four thousand mysteriously reemerges, "If this were a TV mystery, an important clue would pop up at this time and clarify everything."

Chan Is Missing is especially delightful in its gentle subversion of cherished film noir clichés and motifs—the murder weapon, the "other woman," the witness who won't talk, the disembodied voice through the door, the magically reappearing bundle of currency. No bullets or fisticuffs are ever exchanged in Wang's film, however—the closest thing to a serious threat is the female caller who curtly tells Jo to stop asking questions. The protagonists' only threatening actions are Steve's joking, half-hearted gestures to break down the door of a recalcitrant potential witness. A gun turns up but is never fired, and held only once when Jo uncovers it under the taxi cab seat.

Critics gave *Chan Is Missing* mostly high marks; some even compared it to *Citizen Kane*. Vincent Canby hailed it as "a major discovery . . . one of the funniest, most humane, and wisest films I've seen in a very long time, as well as a small miracle of efficient movie-making."[5] *The Village Voice* called it "a valentine, not a dirge, for the collision of cultures,"[6] while the *San Francisco Chronicle* hailed it as "a funny, high-spirited caper . . . far more enjoyable than many slick, predictable whodunits."[7]

Despite wide critical acclaim, however, *Chan Is Missing* failed to kick off a movement of Asian-American independent filmmaking the way Spike Lee's *She's Gotta Have It* did for the African-American filmmaking renaissance of the late eighties and early nineties. This can be attributed, perhaps, to the very diffuse nature of Asian-American culture itself. Some eight years later, Gregg Araki would find a successful niche as an independent filmmaker, not as an Asian-American director but as a leader of the burgeoning "queer" cinema movement of the early nineties. It would be more than a decade before another Chan—Tony—would find acclaim with his Chinese-American independent offering, *Combination Platter*.

Wang went on to make an even more modest indie feature with *Dim Sum: A Little Bit of Heart*. His subsequent foray into mainstream studio production, *Slamdance*, revisited the film noir genre with less-than-sterling results, an unqualified critical and box office bomb. He returned to Chinese and Chinese-American themes with *Eat a Bowl of Tea* in 1990, *Life is Cheap, Toilet Paper is Expensive* in 1992, and the critical and popular success *The Joy Luck Club* in 1993.

In 1995, Wang departed from his usual ethnic subject matter to direct the back-to-back independent features *Smoke* and *Blue in the Face*. Featuring veteran Harvey Keitel and fellow independent Jim Jarmusch among cameos by Lily Tomlin and Madonna, both films revolve around the comings and goings in a Brooklyn tobacco shop. In a move reminiscent of Francis Coppola's twin productions of *The Outsiders* and *Rumble Fish*, Wang decided to make the largely improvisational second film *Blue in the Face* using the same location and some of the same actors: "While we were rehearsing, I kept feeling that we've got to do something with all these wonderful actors who have got small parts. I was constantly feeling, 'There's a lot of energy and talent. Why aren't we doing something more with them?' "[8]

It would seem that Wang is most comfortable when working in the genre of the art film, close to his independent roots. An interviewer once asked Wang if he would accept an offer to do a big Hollywood film. He replied, "I'd do it in a second. I love *Back to the Future*; I love the money that it's made. But I know I'll always come back to whatever I can charge up on my credit card to make a movie that I *really* want to make, even if it's in 16mm again."[9] Despite his eagerness to make blockbuster films, it would seem that Wang's most resonant and honest films are those small pictures with humanistic concerns, particularly those with origins in his Chinese-American heritage. As Wang himself once admitted, "We don't need any more myths."[10]

NOTES

1. Wayne Wang, interview. David Thomson, "Chinese Takeout," *Film Comment*, September-October 1985, p. 25.

2. Ibid., p. 25.

3. Wayne Wang, interview. *American Film*, July-August 1986, p. 17.

4. Richard Patterson, "*Chan Is Missing*, or How to Make a Successful Feature for $22,315.92," *American Cinematographer*, February 1983, p. 33.

5. Vincent Canby, review of *Chan Is Missing*, *New York Times*, May 2, 1982, p. C1.

6. Carrie Rickey, "Some Moving Pictures (and Some That Aren't)," *Village Voice*, April 27, 1982, p. 27.

7. Judy Stone, "A Humorous Treat From Chinatown," *San Francisco Chronicle*, December 12, 1981, p. B3.

8. Connie Benesch, "Twofers in a Brooklyn Smoke Shop," *Los Angeles Times*, July 23, 1995, p. E29.

9. *American Film*, p. 19.

10. Thomson, *Film Comment*, p. 29.

CHAPTER 4

Punk's Progress:
Smithereens
(1982)

USA: Unrated

16mm Color

Running time: 93 minutes

Directed by Susan Seidelman

Cast in alphabetical order:

Susan Berman. . . . . Wren

Joel Brooks. . . . . Xerox Boss

Tom Cherwin. . . . . Mike

Nada Despotovich. . . . . Cecile

Richard Hell. . . . . Eric

Roger Jett. . . . . Billy

D.J. O'Neill. . . . . Ed

Brad Rijn. . . . . Paul

Pamela Speed. . . . . Terry

Kitty Summerall. . . . . Eric's Wife

Robynne White. . . . . Landlady

Cinematography by Chirine El Khadem

Music by
  Glenn Mercer
  Bill Million
Written by
  Peter Askin
  Ron Nyswaner
  Susan Seidelman
Production design by Franz Harlan
Edited by Susan Seidelman
Produced by Susan Seidelman

> My idea was to capture the crazy energy of the rock clubs, the
> sleazy bars, the tenement lofts. I wanted to people the film with
> characters who were products of the mass culture of the 1970's
> and 80's, kids who grew up on rock and roll, fast food, and drugs.
> Susan Seidelman[1]

By the end of the seventies, sixties survivors like the characters depicted in
The Return of the Secaucus Seven had given up the vanguard to a more chaotic
youth movement. The punk rock explosion spearheaded by the Sex Pistols,
the Clash, and others blew away hippie values of peace and love, trans-
forming popular music and fashion while at the same time embracing both
anarchy and crass commercialism.

  With the eighties underway, however, the punk movement that revital-
ized popular music and fashion in Great Britain and the United States since
1976 was on the wane, a casualty of its own self-destructive anarchy. By
1980, punk had all but ceased to be a viable force, giving way to fashion-
conscious New Wave music. Nonetheless, many films made belated attempts to chronicle and cash in on the craze, just as others tried to mine pay
dirt from the sixties counterculture some ten years earlier. Some, such as
The Great Rock 'n Roll Swindle, were sneering, cynical documentaries that
fed upon and regurgitated self-destructive aspects of the doomed movement; others chronicled the music in a more or less straightforward fashion,
as in *The Decline of Western Civilization*. Still other films appropriated punk's
nihilistic attitudes and extruded them into trite narratives, in such "post-
modern" works as *Repo Man* and *Liquid Sky*. One film that did cast an honest
and unflinching eye on the seamy pop subculture was Susan Seidelman's
debut feature, *Smithereens*. Despite its flaws, the film stands as one of the
decade's most insightful documents of a young person's descent into the
dehumanizing punk netherworld.

Smithereens traces a week or so in the life of a feisty nineteen-year-old refugee from New Jersey suburbia named Wren, who has taken up residence in trendy SoHo with aspirations for fame as a rock star. With no apparent talent for singing or playing music, she blithely embarks on a campaign of self-promotion, chasing punk rock singers and plastering photocopied pictures of her face along walls and windows beside the usual bills advertising rock concerts. The shy, quiet portrait artist Paul becomes infatuated with Wren and shares his van with her after she is evicted unceremoniously from her apartment. Wren is uninterested in a relationship with Paul and instead pursues the New Wave singer Eric, whom she wants to manage as a rock act. Eric promises to take her to Los Angeles in his search for a recording contract, but mostly treats her with amused indifference, as he does his other groupies, which include a willowy blonde woman and a feisty brunette who treats him to meals to talk over "business." Wren, in turn, treats Paul in a similarly callous fashion, coming to stay with him only when she finds herself with nowhere else to go. She bounces back and forth between the callous-but-exciting Eric and the warm-but-boring Paul until they both abandon her.

Seidelman's early life did not anticipate her later success as a film director. Born on December 11, 1952, in Abington, Pennsylvania, a suburb of Philadelphia, she admitted in an interview with Peter Golden of *Films in Review* that unlike "all the famous directors who spent their childhoods in the balconies of movie houses, I didn't go to movies much. My idea of a great movie was *The Parent Trap* with Hayley Mills." She became interested in film much later, while studying graphic design at Drexel University. Not one for domestic chores, she tired of the considerable amount of sewing required for the major, explaining that "I switched my major to film because it seemed like an easy way to earn a degree; just watch movies and bluff my way through college."[2]

Considering these frivolous aspirations, it may seem surprising that she would ultimately pursue filmmaking as a profession. Upon graduating from Drexel, however, Seidelman worked as an assistant to the producer of a local television show, and in 1974 she moved to lower Manhattan to attend the Graduate School of Film and Television at New York University. At NYU she slowly became more visually literate,[3] achieving remarkable success as a student filmmaker. Her short film *And You Act Like One, Too* won a Student Academy Award, and a grant from the American Film Institute enabled her to make a second film, *Deficit*. Her third outing, entitled *Yours Truly, Andrea G. Stern*, won several awards at a number of film festivals. Her greatest achievement, however, was still some years off.

In the summer of 1980, three years after earning her master of fine arts degree, Seidelman enlisted other NYU alumni to start production on her first feature film, *Smithereens*. Initially she gathered together a total of $25,000 for the film's budget, gleaned from a $10,000 inheritance and three years of savings earned from freelance editing and work on television commercials. After only two weeks of shooting, however, Seidelman found that the production had already devoured $18,000. Then, during a rehearsal, lead actress Susan Berman fell off a fire escape and broke her leg, delaying shooting for several months. Undaunted, Seidelman used the hiatus to raise an additional $55,000 through a limited partnership set up with friends and relatives. She shot two weeks during the following January, and finished production with a final three weeks in the summer of 1981. All in all, it took two years and approximately $80,000 to get the film in the can.[4]

The movie was a genuine piece of guerrilla filmmaking, as Seidelman "had to sneak into the subway at 2 A.M. and hide the camera in a travel bag, hoping that the subway police wouldn't throw us off the trains." In order to shoot scenes in the Peppermint Lounge nightclub, Seidelman offered to provide a band and three hundred people; the club made money selling drinks at the bar. She worked a similar deal for the cafe scenes: "We knew between seven in the morning and four in the afternoon the cafe doesn't do much business, so we said that if they would let us film there I'd buy the crew—there were maybe 20 people on the set—I'd buy 20 lunches and pay for all the cappuccino or whatever else."[5]

Smithereens' energy and verve did not go unnoticed, and it was selected for "Director's Fortnight," a showcase for new filmmakers' works screened outside the main competition at Cannes. Impressed by the film, director Gilles Jacob decided to place it in the main competition, alongside works by Alan Parker, Wim Wenders, and Costa-Gavras. This was a first for an American independent film. As it turned out, Seidelman found herself the only American *and* the only female director in competition in this most prestigious of festivals.

The film opens as a pair of checkered sunglasses dangling in slow motion are suddenly plucked from its owner's hand by a young woman dressed in a houndstooth skirt and fishnet stockings. The woman, Wren, runs down the stairs to the subway, posting pictures of herself (which read "Who is this girl?"). She takes a seat on the subway across from a shy young man, Paul. Attracted, Paul follows Wren off the train. She turns into a photocopy shop, where a man can be seen to bark orders at her through the glass window.

A title sequence shows the passing of the day, as the same street scene dissolves a number of times to end at dusk. Outside, Paul waits for her. Walking with her, he asks her name, but Wren simply gives him a Xerox, refusing to speak to him.

At the Peppermint Lounge, a punk hangout, Wren struts into the club past the waiting line and bouncer, who yells after her despite her claim to be "on the guest list." People dance while Wren watches the band's singer. When the band takes a break, she joins him at a crowded table, only to be ignored as he dawdles with his groupies. "Remember me? I think you're really great," Wren tells him. Wren leaves the club in disgust after her rebuff, and Paul waits for her outside. He walks her to her apartment, asking her for a date. "Where'd you say you were from again?" she asks. "Montana." he replies.

Wren sneaks down the hall and up the stairs of her apartment house. She kicks off a TV playing the national anthem, as a woman in a white brassiere sleeps on the floor nearby.

An alarm clock awakens Paul, who has been sleeping in a van parked in a trash-strewn lot. He stares at the photocopy of Wren, as a photo of a girl peeks out behind him. Sitting in the front seat, he plays a tape and retrieves some personal articles from the glove box; inside we see a gun. As he shaves, a man appears at the driver-side window, asking him to sell his vehicle. Paul declines the offer and the man disappears.

Night again. Paul waits at the front door of Wren's apartment. When she comes out he reminds her that they have a date. Wren is short and rude to him, but he persists in walking with her. When he suggests a movie, she pauses and consents.

In a movie theater, a cheap black-and-white horror movie unreels. On the screen, a man corners a frightened woman and puts some kind of monstrous louse on her neck; she retaliates, burying a pair of scissors in his right eye. Unfazed by the onscreen gore and silliness, Paul sheepishly tries to put an arm around Wren.

Outside the movie theater, Paul tries to interest Wren in further activities, when a scene distracts them. A young man exits a cab, leaving a distraught young woman who shouts after him as the taxi drives away. Wren is immediately attracted to the young man, aspiring punk singer and musician Eric.

Later at a cafe, Wren attempts to win Eric's affections with idle chatter, while Paul plays a video game. Paul asks Wren to speak with him in private, while Eric slicks back his hair with beer. Wren wants five more minutes so she can "make a connection." Dejected, Paul drinks some water from the sink in the bathroom, and exits to see Wren dancing with Eric. The pay phone rings as he departs, and he takes it off the hook.

Eric carries a laughing Wren over his shoulder through the door of his trashy apartment. "Hey, you're gonna wake up the rats," he chides. While *Breakfast for Bonzo* plays on the television, Eric sings "All the Way." A poster featuring Eric and the name of his band "Smithereens" festoons a wall. Wren checks out his record album, while Eric brings a couple of beers and talks about his plans to get a record deal in Los Angeles.

Brushing her teeth in the background, Wren stumbles upon Eric's roommate, an androgynous poseur decked in ludicrous New Wave attire—red pants, low neck shirt, and red-colored hair. "Hey, you want to make it with me first?" he asks pathetically. "Don't make me sick," she scowls.

Wren finds Eric asleep in bed when she returns and she tries to wake him with a kiss. "Hey, wake up." He continues sleeping. She rubs his shoulder, and ponders what to do. Fade out.

A pair of legs in a red dress paces in the room, then sits on a stool as a religious program plays on the TV. Wren lies in bed with Eric, when the obnoxious roommate sidles up and tries to kiss her. The legs belong to the blonde woman first seen in the taxi with Eric. She appears to be waiting.

Morning. "Got a lot of people to talk to, get ready for when I go," explains Eric. Wren gets out of the bed, and the roommate beckons the blonde to join him in bed. Wren sits eating from a jar of peanut butter, and Eric enters to brush his teeth. Wren tells him about a dream about an earthquake in California. He rebuffs her offer to make him breakfast, "I can open something." "I'm in a hurry." He primps in front of a mirror, stopping to kiss her and ask her name.

Wren trudges back to her apartment through a wasteland of graffiti and garbage. Arriving at the lime-green facade of her building, she deftly evades the landlady, only to find her room padlocked. The landlady refuses Wren entry into the apartment until she pays four months' back rent. Wren asks for her clothes, and the landlady tells her to wait outside.

A little girl sets up a three-card monte while Wren's clothes come showering down, followed by a drenching bucket of water.

Wren visits her sister in a New Jersey suburb, where her niece suns herself on a lawn chair. Her sister appears with curlers and a bikini revealing a slouchy pot belly. Wren tells her sad tale when her brother-in-law shouts for dinner. "You can be as nice as you want, but you're not getting any money," he tells Wren as he polishes his car. "Thanks for reminding me what it's like to be related to an asshole," she spits back and leaves.

Paul starts his engine, and begins driving away as Wren arrives suitcase and TV in hand, pleading with him to stop for her. She runs in front of the car, he stops, and then runs around and gets in the back of the van. Paul orders her to get out, but when he tries to resume driving, his car won't start. She stands waiting in his rearview mirror.

That night Paul helps Wren break into her flat, with stockings over their faces, rousing the landlady's poodle. They get away with some of her belongings, but Wren falls, scraping her legs.

In the van later Paul daubs her scraped thigh with iodine. Wren toys with Paul's gun. He tells her that his dad gave it to him, thinking he might need it in New York. She gleefully reads a letter he wrote to a Maryann, teasing him about it.

Paul ignites a fire in a trash can, and they sit beside it on an old bench seat. Wren sleeps beside Paul in the back of the van, while he tries to peek down her top, looking upon her intently.

Morning brings the din of jackhammers. Wren paints her name and a line in red spray paint across a building facade to a posted picture of her face.

Having invited herself unannounced into Eric's apartment, Wren sits on a mattress and tears the image of the blonde woman out of Eric's photos of them as a couple, burning them with a match. When Eric arrives with blonde in tow, he berates Wren for her selfish intrusion. She leaves in a huff, and oddly, Eric follows after to retrieve her in the night streets.

Paul sits up in the front seat of his van. Someone appears at the window, and thinking it's Wren, he opens the door. It is a streetwalker, who asks to sit for a while inside in the warmth of the cab. She offers various sex acts for money, but Paul sheepishly declines. She tells him her pimp wants to buy the van.

A photocopier sorts copies, as Wren reads a magazine article entitled "Those Who Died Young." The television blasts a program of destruction: "Disasters . . . The next victim could be you." A poster on the wall reads "Stop Nuclear Power."

At a friend, Cecile's, apartment, Wren sings Eric's song "Here He Comes Again." Wren plays the record loud, dancing; Cecile takes pictures of herself with a Polaroid camera. Cecile exhorts her to stop: "The people downstairs hate us." Wren clowns, holding an open *Playboy* centerfold up to her chest. She speaks glowingly of Eric: "He's not nice, he's great." Cecile mentions that her parents want her to move back to Ohio. Wren asks Cecile if she can stay at her flat, but Cecile politely declines, citing roommate difficulties. Cecile asks about getting her a date with one of Eric's friends. Wren calls Eric, gets the roommate. "OK, tell him I'm coming," Wren tells him and leaves with Cecile as the phonograph plays "Here He Comes Again."

At Eric's flat, Cecile sits with Billy, who asks if she would like to join him in a bath. "Got any bubbles?" she asks. Billy pulls out a bottle of dishwashing soap, "This be OK?"

Wren grows impatient waiting for Eric, and leaves with Cecile. Disillusioned, she returns to Paul's van, curling up beside him, still dressed in a short skirt, seamed stockings and green blouse. Paul awakens and goes up to the front cab to sleep. Paul shouts at Wren, "Just come in whenever you want to, whenever you can't find someone else to take you in. " He tells her that he will leave New York in seven days.

Her stockinged legs striding under the untucked tales of a man's dress shirt, Wren hurries to Eric's apartment. Eric's roommate Billy (now sporting blue-brown hair) first ignores her, then reveals that Eric has gone to take a "business" meeting at Cafe Orleans.

Eric is having lunch with a self-assured woman who talks of investors for his music ventures. She tells him to order anything he wants, and excuses herself. Wren enters and sits at his table, greeting the nonplused Eric: "Long time no see." Wren talks of them getting a mobile home in LA when the woman returns. Wren thoughtlessly gives the woman an order for food, and she tells Wren to get out of her seat. Wren throws Pepsi in the woman's face and the two tussle on the cafe floor.

That night, some hookers proposition Paul as he carries his art supplies back to his van. The pimp asks again if Paul wants to sell the van. He answers no, while one of the prostitutes teases "Hey, baby, I got something to sell." Inside the van, Paul finds Wren bundled up, nursing a bloody lip. "All a bunch of creeps," she broods, "everybody's trying so hard to be cool, and they're all a bunch of big zeros. Paul, you know why I came back here tonight? Because I missed you." Paul reminds her of his plan to leave for New Hampshire. "What am I supposed to do," she asks, "sleep on the subway?" "I was sort of hoping you'd come with me," Paul replies earnestly. Wren looks off.

Wren shoots her spray can aimlessly, looking listless and bored. She goes to the van looking for Paul, and instead discovers Eric sitting in the front seat. "Surprise!" he says, "It took me two hours to find this place." "How's your friend, the lady wrestler?" Wren replies. Eric asks if she owns the van, and tells her the LA trip is off because he's broke. Wren tells him she's going to New Hampshire. Eric, however, has a plan to get money for the LA trip.

In a cocktail lounge, a singer belts out a flat rendition of "Copacabana" while Wren, uncharacteristically dolled up, sits and laughs with a middle-aged balding man named Ed. Eric, meanwhile, sits smirking at the bar; when a woman asks for a light, he rudely throws her the matchbook without even a glance. Wren kisses Ed on the cheek and suggests going back to his hotel.

Ed and Wren enter a cab, where Ed can't wait to awkwardly paw and kiss her. Eric unexpectedly enters from the other door, threatening Ed with Paul's gun. Eric takes Ed's wallet, jewelry, and watch, and forces him to remove and hand over his pants. Wren and Eric leave the frightened victim in the cab to drive on, and repair back to Eric's flat to count their booty.

"What part of LA do you want to live in?" Wren asks. "Malibu," replies Eric. "I just want to be in a swimming pool, eating tacos, and signing autographs, that's all," Wren says wistfully. Fade out.

Fade in to Paul sitting in the rear door of his van, huddling under a blanket. Wren returns to collect her belongings leaving her television with him, telling him, "Vermont is gonna seem pretty dull after all this."

Paul lectures her: "You can't keep doing this forever, You can't just go and use people, and when you're done with them you go use somebody else. All you want to think about is yourself. Well, other people got feelings too, don't you know that?" Wren confesses that she can't be happy in New Hampshire, admitting, "I don't even like trees."

Wren trudges upstairs to Eric's flat, knocking and calling out to him. The blonde sits on the stairs, and tells Wren that Eric drove off earlier. Wren denies it, cursing. The blonde offers her a drag on her cigarette. Wren takes it and joins her on the stairs.

BLONDE WOMAN: You were going to LA with him?

WREN: Yeah, and he's got all my money.

BLONDE WOMAN: He owes lots of people money. The day we met I lent him six hundred bucks.

WREN: I was gonna manage his group.

BLONDE WOMAN: I was going to do that once too.

WREN: So what happened?

BLONDE WOMAN: Same thing that happened to you.

WREN: Were you his girl friend for a long time?

BLONDE WOMAN: Just for a couple of weeks—then we got married.

WREN: He never told me he was married.

WREN: He's really fucked, isn't he?

BLONDE WOMAN: Life is fucked.

Wren goes to Cecile's apartment, but her roommate won't let her in. Cecile goes out in the hallway to talk. "Why don't you stay with Paul?" she asks. "I'm tired of living in a van," Wren spits back and leaves in a flurry of denunciations.

Wren returns to the Peppermint Lounge, and sneaks past the line again. This time the bouncer follows after her as she roams the floor, with bags in hand. She comes up and sits on the keys of a piano punk singer, "X-cessive." As he plays, she tries to interest him in her. The bouncer catches her and ejects her violently from the club.

Wren calls her sister from a phone booth, but instead reaches her boorish brother-in-law and hangs up the phone. She rides the subway, and trudges aimlessly through the streets of New York, finally returning to Paul's van. Arriving at the van breathless, she talks to the feet protruding from under the front of the van. The familiar pimp emerges, cursing the $700 paid for a "piece of shit that doesn't even work." She opens the back of the van to discover a group of hookers sitting inside beneath Paul's portrait of her. As one of the women reads aloud a magazine article about the marriage of Candice Bergen to Louis Malle, Wren picks up her TV and walks out into the littered landscape.

Walking down a bridge Wren is accosted by a passing motorist in a convertible, who repeatedly propositions her: "Got a better place to spend your time?" Ignoring him at first, she wearily pauses and turns her head, and the frame freezes.

End credits roll over a closing song: "You must be waiting for something to happen, maybe something will happen, but nothing ever happens."

Women directors have traditionally been an anomaly in the American movie industry. Although thousands of women worked in Hollywood before 1960 as screenwriters, editors, and art directors, only a handful of female directors are remembered today—Alice Guy-Blache in the early years, Lois Weber in the period following the First World War, Dorothy Arzner in the thirties and forties, and Ida Lupino for a brief time following World War II. The women's movement in the 1970s did little to alter the prepondance of male power in the movie industry, but the decade did see an increasing number of women emerge as screenwriters, producers, and directors. Although some sensitive films were made (e. g., Joan Micklin Silver's ethnic period piece *Hester Street*, Claudia Weill's perceptive *Girlfriends*), many women found a niche directing pictures in the commercial teen-film genre. Martha Coolidge (who started her career as a documentarist) received critical raves for her *Valley Girl* while Amy Heckerling embarked on a lucrative if critically inconsequential string of films with *Fast Times at Ridgemont High*.[6]

Seidelman arrived on the scene at a time when few female directors were making successful mainstream films about adult women living out their own experiences. For her next four pictures, Seidelman would consistently mine familiar territory—the suburban refugee who becomes a city girl, caught up in the excitement and chaos of the urban environment. Her "girl in the city" was nothing like the Marlo Thomas "That Girl" archetype, who repeatedly took shelter under the wing of urbane beau Donald Hollanger. The Seidelman protagonist was a tough, if naïve, woman making her way on her own terms in the big world. As such, Wren was the first of the filmmaker's heroines to display the typical Seidelman characteristics. She is a streetwise but untutored waif, a *Riot Grrrl* precursor in her red high-top sneakers, seamed stockings, and short dresses. She scorns the bourgeois life of her sister and brother-in-law, and takes to the streets in New York looking for fame and kicks in the East Village punk scene. Her lipsticked mouth wears a permanent scowl as she trudges the streets of lower Manhattan looking for her next scam.

Wren's often unsympathetic character is intentionally abrasive, according to Seidelman, who wanted a female protagonist "who had a lot of energy but wouldn't necessarily always be nice." Seidelman wanted to buck two prevailing female role models in Hollywood movies: the sex symbol and the maternal type.[7] She also compared Wren to the Ratso Rizzo character in John Schlesinger's *Midnight Cowboy* (1969): "charming but also a liar." Wren is streetwise and comically pathetic in a fashion somewhat reminiscent of Ratso, but unlike Dustin Hoffman's heartwrenching characterization, Susan Berman's character exudes little charm. Her antics may be amusing and even vicariously intriguing, as when she burns photographs of Eric's girlfriend in his own apartment or cruelly helps him dupe, rob, and "pants" a harmless lecher. Ultimately, she elicits audience sympathy only when she herself becomes a victim. This vulnerability is palpable, almost heartbreaking, when she elbows her way into the Peppermint Lounge to ingratiate herself with an oafish punk singer who simply ignores her. She is childlike in her offers to make breakfast ("I could open something," she tells him) for Eric in an attempt to persuade him not to leave his flat. She is most endearing when she retreats to the shelter of Paul's van, after being put upon by the world at large, whether fondled as a sex object by Eric's boorish roommate or pummeled by his female "business" associate. She is never truly likable, however, and hence problematic as a protagonist; any empathy for her comes mostly in the form of pity, a response to her failed attempts to manipulate others. Thus, Wren is ultimately a powerless character, behaving in a fashion very much like her namesake, her energy spent flitting aimlessly from place to place.

The two films have in common the trashy New York cityscape as a backdrop to their respective stories, and indeed, *Smithereens* goes several steps beyond *Cowboy* in its depressingly accurate depictions of the rubble-strewn landscape of lower Manhattan. Seidelman shares Schlesinger's glee in strewing her film with sidelong references to pop culture's shrine, the television set, as monitors in various locations spew scenes from Ronald Reagan's chimp-flick *Bedtime for Bonzo*, late-night broadcasts of the national anthem, and documentary scenes of destruction under an announcer's voice that proclaims "The next victim could be you," all recalling the mocking, banal television images that waft through *Cowboy*.

On closer inspection, however, the restless heroine of *Smithereens* might be better compared with the protagonist of an earlier Schlesinger film, the cynical Swinging London satire *Darling*. Schlesinger's film may have a more attractive and sympathetic protagonist in Julie Christie's Diana Scott than Susan Berman's Wren, but both women bounce back and forth between the archetypal stable, loving, but ultimately boring "nice guy" and the exciting but irresponsible, egotistical "bad boy," who turns out to be even more manipulative and rapacious than the protagonist herself. But where Julie Christie's Diana had a beguiling charm to offset her maddening capriciousness, Susan Berman's Wren has only shallow abrasiveness to offer the viewer. And where Diana was a glamorous model, Wren is a disheveled, even slovenly, waif of the streets. Diana becomes a genuine success at the top of her profession, whereas Wren fails even at her attempts as an obsequious groupie. Ultimately Diana finds herself secure and physically comfortable, but stranded in a domestic limbo of boredom and loneliness; Wren seems destined to an urban hell of homelessness on the filthy streets of New York.

Seidelman has characterized *Smithereens* as a disinterested, objective look at selected representatives of a pop subculture, yet what many critics liked least about the film was what they perceived to be the director's moral judgments about the characters and their behavior. Pauline Kael complained in *The New Yorker* that Wren's escapades "were fun to watch until the picture started using her as a bad example. The movie didn't just set her up as a victim of false ideals; it also delivered the homiletic message that if you're not kind to other people you'll be left alone. . . . *Smithereens* is one of those dismally naive movies that make you pay for every smile or chuckle you had at the start."[8] Richard Corliss wrote that *"Smithereens* has the judgmental attitudes of a Hollywood *'expose'* with little of the craft,"[9] while Ira Mayer concurred that the lead character was so self-serving and solipsistic that "a feeble last-minute attempt at moralizing becomes merely laughable."[10] One reviewer went so far as to condemn *Smithereens* for its tacit message "that prostitution awaits all women who transgress the bourgeois codes" of accepted social behavior.

Paul, whose character emerges simultaneously with that of Wren, represents the old-style values that began to unravel and disintegrate in the decade of punk. Seidelman described him as "an earthling that goes to Mars and suddenly finds himself in this world where the rules of his world are no longer operative." He is, in fact, a model of the sixties: an artist who yearns to leave the ugly city for the pristine beauty of New Hampshire (where former sixties activists of John Sayles's *Secaucus Seven* gathered to take personal inventory). Wren, on the other hand, wants nothing less than to "be in a swimming pool, eating tacos, and signing autographs," confessing, "I don't even like trees."

The success of *Smithereens* brought Seidelman a flurry of screenplays, most of them directed at the teen market. She judiciously passed on all of them. However, when producers Midge Sanford and Sarah Pillsbury sent her a script written by Leora Barish entitled *Desperately Seeking Susan*, Seidelman was enthralled: "I'm very superstitious, and when I first heard the title I took it as an omen. And the second thing is that it dealt with two worlds—one was kind of East Village bohemian, people kind of living on the fringes. . . . And the other half of the script was about suburbia, which is where I come from." The film, about a bored New Jersey housewife who is mistaken for a trendy seductress with a contract out on her life, featured Rosanna Arquette and a rising pop singer, Madonna Ciccone, whose popularity coincidentally skyrocketed during the making of the film, ensuring a healthy box office. The success of the film, which drew generally favorable reviews and earned back six times its production cost of $5 million, encouraged Orion to offer Seidelman a three-picture contract. Predictably, other independents vilified her for selling out to Hollywood. In an article reeking of sour grapes, Jon Jost wrote that she jumped "from self-proclaimed 'guerrilla filmmaking' to 40-foot trailers" with *Desperately Seeking Susan*, while Jim Jarmusch dismissed the film openly in an interview appearing in *American Film*.

Desperately Seeking Susan marked a shift in direction for Seidelman, away from the unflinching realism of *Smithereens* toward fantasy and screwball comedy, a genre that she has exploited with increasingly uneven and disappointing results. Her next film, *Making Mr. Right*, unsuccessfully attempted to explore the dilemma of the contemporary career woman—

juggling career and love or family life—through a mix of science fiction and comedy. Critics panned the effort mercilessly. Her next film, *Cookie* (1989), took a comedic look at the gangster genre, and was similarly ineffective both critically and commercially. Seidelman's greatest disaster, however, came with the last of her pictures for Orion, an adaptation of the successful Fay Weldon novel *The Life and Loves of a She-Devil*. Seidelman again tried to champion a feminist point of view through unsophisticated humor. Critics pounced on the film and tore it to shreds; Stanley Kaufmann spoke for many when he labeled the movie "an abysmal piece of junk."

Seidelman appeared to sustain serious damage from this latest round of practically universal criticism. In any event, she would not direct another feature for several years, and worked sporadically on such pieces as a British-funded documentary about her high school friends and a short film contribution to the feature-length compendium *Erotic Tales*, a group effort which brought together shorts from such directors as Bob Rafelson and Melvin Van Peebles.

Seidelman emerged as a heroine of independent filmmaking in the early and mid-eighties, at a time when other women in film found their heads bumping against the industry's glass ceiling. Some, like director-cinematographer Claudia Weill (*Girlfriends*), turned their energies to television projects. Others, such as Joyce Chopra (*Smooth Talk*), made auspicious independent debuts only to wither under the pressure of studio-financed film production (*Bright Lights, Big City*). Others such as Joan Micklin Silver (*Hester Street*) and Martha Coolidge (*Valley Girl*) persevered and ultimately found small respectable niches making specialty films. And successful women directors like Amy Heckerling and Penelope Spheeris digressed from promising early works (*Fast Times at Ridgemont High*, *The Decline of Western Civilization*) to crank out dispensable fare such as *Look Who's Talking* and *The Beverly Hillbillies*. Ironically, as Seidelman saw her career slide in the 1990s, other mainstream women directors such as Penny Marshall have found lucrative careers.

In retrospect, Seidelman seemed to succumb to the fate she originally tried to avoid earlier in her career: the consequences of selecting inappropriate projects. At the height of her directing career, in a interview with Janet Maslin of the *New York Times*, she confided: "I didn't want to make a turkey movie, just jump into something and wind up cutting my career short before it even got started."[11] But it was her succession of "turkey movies" that, more than anything else, contributed to her career stall. Sadly, Seidelman is often left out of any serious discussion concerning pioneering independents of the 1980s, such as Jarmusch, Lee, Sayles, and the Coens. Her languishing career can perhaps be attributed to her inability to script original work, combined with her tendency to uncritically accept the often inferior projects offered by members of the Hollywood establishment. In a decade that has seen the remarkable comeback of many assumed has-been industry players (for example, John Travolta's remarkable return to quality pictures after his role in Quentin Tarantino's smash hit *Pulp Fiction*), it is much too soon to write off the talented and resilient Susan Seidelman.

NOTES

1. Annette Insdorf, " *'Smithereens'*—The Story of a Cinderella Movie," *New York Times*, May 8, 1982, p. B1.

2. Susan Seidelman, interview. Peter Golden, *Films in Review*, June-July 1985, p. 51.

3. In an interview with Michelle Green of *People* magazine (April 29, 1985), Seidelman admitted that "I was intimidated. Everybody else had seen fifty billion German expressionist movies, so I started going to five or six movies a week to catch up."

4. Susan Seidelman, interview. Richare Patterson, "An Interview with Susan Seidelman on the Making of *Smithereens,*" *American Cinematographer*, May 1983, p. 70.

5. Ibid., p. 70.

6. Robert Sklar, *Film: An International History of the Medium* (New York: Abrams, 1994) pp. 104, 474.

7. Patterson, "Smithereens," p. 224.

8. Pauline Kael, *The New Yorker*, April 22, 1985, p. 58.

9. Richard Corliss, *Time*, March 14, 1983, p. 90.

10. Ira Mayer, *New York Post*, November 19, 1992, p. 43.

11. Susan Seidelman, interview. Janet Maslin, *New York Times*, March 22, 1985, p. C1.

Deadpan Alley:
Stranger Than Paradise
(1984)

USA/West Germany

Rating: R

35mm Black and White

Produced by: Zweites Deutsches Fernsehen (ZDF)
Cinesthesia Productions Inc.

Grokenberger Film Produktion

Running time: 89 minutes

Directed by Jim Jarmusch

Cast in order of appearance:

John Lurie. . . . . Willie

Ezster Balint. . . . . Eva

Richard Edson. . . . . Eddie

Cecillia Stark. . . . . Aunt Lotte

Danny Rosen. . . . . Billy

Tom DiCillo. . . . . Airline Agent

Richard Boes. . . . . Factory Worker

Rockets Redglare. . . . . Poker Player

Harvey Perr. . . . . Poker Player

Brian J. Burchill. . . . . Poker Player

Sara Driver. . . . . Girl with Hat

Paul Sloane. . . . . Motel Owner

Tom DiCillo. . . . . Airline Agent

Ramellzee. . . . . Man with the Money

Cinematography by Tom DiCillo

Music by John Lurie

Written by Jim Jarmusch

Production designed by

Matt Buchwald

Guido Chiesa

Sam Edwards

Tom Jarmusch

Una McClure

Louis Tancredi

Stephen Torton

Edited by

Jim Jarmusch

Melody London

Produced by

Sara Driver

Otto Grokenberger

> If aliens watched us make a film, they would think we were
> ridiculous. We spend all this money running this material that's
> sensitive to light, because it has silver alloys in it, through
> antiquated machinery. Then we edit it and spend all this time in
> a little room putting it together to imitate life. . . . And for what?
> Why don't we just go outside and watch real life instead?
>
> Jim Jarmusch[1]

Two years after the success of *Smithereens*, one of the definitive, most original independent films of the decade arose again from the New York street scene, this time in the form of Jim Jarmusch's *Stranger Than Paradise*. This wryly humorous and picaresque film, in the tradition of the "underground" works of John Cassavetes and Andy Warhol, became one of the first art films to transcend its cult status and become a cause célèbre for independents and a classic film in its own right.

Jarmusch has professed as much interest in the "world cinema" of European and Japanese filmmakers as in the tradition of American movies. He is also perhaps the most idiosyncratic and autonomous of the eighties independents. He turned down numerous American studio offers after the success of *Stranger* in order to maintain complete creative control as well as ownership of his negatives, a privilege shared by few other directors. Jarmusch is more than happy to get his funding overseas to ensure that he owns at least half his film, even with the tradeoff of limited distribution and budget constraints that would give many directors pause: "I want to have complete control over my work and I want to make small steps. I don't want to jump into something over my head. I don't want to work with a union crew or have someone telling me how to cut my film or who's going to be cast in it."[2]

Stranger Than Paradise centers on two drolly inert bohemians who, rather than bother themselves with work, while away their time in New York's Lower East Side playing cards, watching television, gambling on race-horses, smoking Chesterfields, and eating TV dinners. The surprise arrival of a young Hungarian girl (cousin to one of them) shatters their idyll of slothfulness and spurs them to far-flung adventures in Cleveland and Florida.

Having fully assimilated himself into the New York scene of artists and musicians, it may surprise some that Jim Jarmusch was born in 1953, not in the Big Apple but in the rubber tire capital of the nation, Akron, Ohio. He watched Japanese horror movies and James Bond pictures as a boy, but Charles Laughton's nightmarish fairytale *The Night of the Hunter* and *Thunder Road* made particularly lasting impressions. His few happy memories of Akron include regular sightings of the Goodyear blimp, otherwise he remembers his hometown as "prefabricated, very ugly. Growing up in Ohio was just planning to get out."[3]

He did get out to New York City, and attended Columbia University as an undergraduate, studying English under noted professors David Shapiro and Kenneth Koch—major literary figures of the so-called New York School of avant-garde poets. He spent much time reading "post-post-structural fiction and the deconstructed narrative and all that stuff," as he told one interviewer.[4]

In 1975, during his final semester at Columbia, Jarmusch traveled to Paris, where he had his first brush with "world cinema" through the archives of the Cinematheque Française. An entire world, heretofore unknown, opened to him, as he explained in a *New York Times* interview:

That's where I saw things I had only read about and heard about—films by many of the good Japanese directors, like Imamura, Ozu, Mizoguchi. Also, films by European directors like Bresson and Dreyer, and even American films, like a retrospective of Samuel Fuller's films, which I only knew from seeing a few of them on television late at night.[5]

Jarmusch returned to New York and enrolled in film studies at New York University, where he became an assistant to the maverick fifties film director Nicholas Ray. He also met the noted New German Cinema director Wim Wenders and worked as a production assistant on his film *Lightning Over Water*, a documentary examining Ray's struggles against cancer. As a result of this experience, along with encouragement from Ray and fellow independent Amos Poe, Jarmusch decided to make a career of filmmaking.

In 1979, about two weeks after Ray's death, Jarmusch used a fellowship grant intended for his tuition and started work on his first production, *Permanent Vacation*, a $15,000 film about "two and a half days in the life of a young guy who doesn't really have any ambitions or responsibility. He doesn't live anywhere specifically. He doesn't go to school; he doesn't work."[6] His professors were unhappy with *Permanent Vacation*'s "excessive" eighty-minute length, but the film found limited exposure on the art film circuit in Europe. According to Jarmusch, the film "really didn't do anything" in the United States.

With one feature under his belt, Jarmusch set about writing the script for a short film he called *Stranger Than Paradise*.[7] Chris Sievernich, executive producer of Wim Wenders' films, was sufficiently impressed with *Permanent Vacation* to give Jarmusch forty minutes of raw black-and-white film stock. Jarmusch filmed the short in a single weekend in February 1982. Jarmusch's script revolved around two humorous deadbeats: the laconic Willie and his dim friend, Eddie, who do little but gamble on cards and horses and watch TV in Willie's dingy Lower East Side flat. The pair find their complacent lives shaken up, however, when Willie's young cousin Eva unexpectedly arrives from Hungary to spend ten days with him before traveling on to stay with her Aunt Lotte in Cleveland.

Jarmusch (who knew a number of musicians from his stint in a band known as the Del-Byzantines) cast Lounge Lizards saxophonist John Lurie as the dour hipster Willy, actor Richard Edson as the amiable Eddie, and Ezster Balint from New York's Squat Theater as the sweet, stubborn Eva. Jarmusch was able to make a thirty-minute film from forty minutes of stock by framing each scene as a continuous long take, shooting none of the conventional closeups, medium shots, reverse shots, and inserts that directors use to increase editing options and relieve the monotony of sequence shots. In order to preserve a sense of continuity within what was essentially a succession of master scenes, Jarmusch interspersed a few seconds of black leader between each shot, effectively separating them from one another and simultaneously giving the film a unique and unusual sense of style. Musing later about Jarmusch's unorthodox approach to filmmaking, Lurie remarked, "I personally thought he was out of his mind."[8]

While editing the film, Jarmusch sensed that *Stranger Than Paradise* could be expanded to feature length by adding two additional "chapters." In addition to the original thirty-minute segment ("The New World") where Willie and Eddie reluctantly welcome Eva into their lives, Jarmusch wrote two more acts—"One Year Later," where Willie and Eddie win $600 in a crooked poker game and trek to wintry Cleveland to visit Eva, and "Paradise," which found the trio traveling to Florida, which oddly bears a strange resemblance to Ohio. The film won the international critics prize at the Rotterdam Film Festival. Jarmusch, buoyed by this success, traveled around Europe looking for investors for his feature. Ultimately, he attracted the attention of Otto Grokenberger, an influential young German producer, who agreed to finance the film.[9]

Jarmusch started shooting the remainder of *Stranger Than Paradise* in January 1984, turning a short film that had cost $8,000 into one that would ultimately run to $120,000. By March, however, Jarmusch had a finished film and was able to show it to a Cannes Film Festival official, who included it in the highly selective film competition. The film ultimately won the Camera d'Or at Cannes for best feature film, took top prize at the Locarno (Switzerland) Film Festival, and made the program of the exclusive New York Film Festival. The film was hailed an offbeat gem by many critics, who praised its deadpan charm and wit.

The film opens with a simple black title card, "Stranger Than Paradise," recalling the similarly stark opening credit of Welles's *Citizen Kane*. Another title appears, identifying this segment of the film as "The New World."

The sound of jet noise precedes a long shot of a young woman dressed all in black, Eva, holding a bag in each hand, standing in a wasteland overlooking an airstrip. As one airliner sits on the ground, another lands; the woman walks out of frame as a string quartet plays plaintive music. Actors' credits appear.

A low angle shot of a spartan flat interior. A lanky man wearing a fedora, Willie, enters and answers the telephone: it is his Hungarian Aunt Lotte, telling him to expect a ten-day visit from his cousin Eva, who is to arrive today.

Eva trudges to a stop on a deserted New York street; she pulls a tape player out of her bag and plays a Screamin' Jay Hawkins's song, "I Put a Spell on You." She continues on down the largely desolate New York environs, past closed storefronts, turning a corner.

The sound of knocking rouses Willie from his bed, and he brusquely welcomes Eva into his cramped apartment. When Eva explains that she will travel on to Cleveland tomorrow, Willie tells her that Aunt Lotte has had to enter a hospital for ten days, so she must stay with him in New York for the time.

Eva, in striped pajamas, smokes and stares out the window when the phone rings. Willie will not be roused, so Eva answers and takes a message from a "Korguy." Willie awakens and hearing her message, then warns her not to answer the phone anymore. He admonishes her not to go out alone, but she goes out the door anyway.

Eva fidgets at the dining table while Willie digs into a TV dinner. Eva is curious, but unimpressed with this American food. Willie doesn't care and devours the meal.

Eva is sitting on the bed when Willie greets a visitor, the gregarious if dim Eddie, who looks to be the smaller twin of Willie. Eva tells him of her plans to go to Cleveland. He tells her Cleveland is a "beautiful city," but admits having never been there. He and Willie are going to the horseraces, but although Eddie invites Eva to tag along, Willie forbids it. Eddie seems to like Eva, who slouches on the bed in boredom after they depart.

Watching a game on TV, Willie tries unsuccessfully to explain the excitement of football to Eva, which she dismisses as "stupid."

Now nighttime, the pair continue to sit before the box, as the music of a sci-fi B-movie plays.

Morning sun plays on the wall while Eva continues watching the tube, as the sounds of slide whistle, clarinet, and vaudevillian dialogue suggest a vintage cartoon.

As Willie dawdles over a newspaper, Eva complains of the dirt and asks if he has a vacuum cleaner. Before she begins to vacuum the room, Willie advises her to first refer to the act in the proper terminology: "choking the alligator."

Willie amuses himself by playing solitaire. When Eva comes home and produces shoplifted canned goods, a carton of Chesterfields, and a TV dinner from inside her overcoat, Willie bestows his begrudging admiration.

Eva does a shuffling dance in the kitchen to the sounds of Screamin' Jay Hawkins, but when Willie arrives he expresses his disapproval and shuts off the music. "It's Screamin' Jay Hawkins and he's a wild man, so bug off," she replies in her deadpan voice. Willie has a gift for Eva—a white patterned dress that she finds "ugly." Eva promises to try it on, but throws it aside.

True to her word, Eva wears the dress as she packs her bags to leave. Willie now is clearly sad to see her go. Without leaving his flat, he bids her farewell and leans pensively against the door.

Outside on the street, Eva stops to pull off the offensive garment and throw it into a convenient garbage can. Eddie appears and the two exchange goodbyes before she walks off down the dark street.

Eddie joins Willie in the flat and they silently drink cans of beer.

A title appears: "One Year Later."

Willie and Eddie are playing poker with three other men. Willie produces a full house. One of the men accuses the pair of cheating; indignant, Eddie and Willie leave in a huff. Down the hall, Willie stops to count their haul for the night, and asks Eddie if they can borrow a car from his brother-in-law, Max.

Willie and Eddie drive through the streets of New York. Willie wonders if the car will make it to Cleveland. They stop to ask a man where Cleveland is. Unsuccessful finding directions, they drive on.

Out on the open road, they gloat over their winnings—$600. The weather gets worse as they cross Pennsylvania, while Eddie marvels drolly at Willie's Hungarian background: "I thought you were an American.... Does Cleveland look a little bit like Budapest?" Willie impatiently tells him to "shut up." The trip drags on through the ugly industrial rust belt.

Willie and Eddie drive through a Cleveland suburb, pulling up before Aunt Lotte's modest bungalow. Aunt Lotte welcomes the pair in her odd Hungarian accent. Speaking Hungarian, she asks if the two are hungry; she brings them borscht. Sitting down in her chair, she explains to Willie in Hungarian that Eva is working at a "hot dog stand."

Willie and Eddie go to meet Eva at the restaurant to surprise her, and she is pleased to see them. Willie doesn't like the neon atmosphere of the place, so they go outside to wait for her to finish her work. A bearded would-be suitor, Billy, walks her out and asks her to see a movie with him. She bids him goodnight and leaves with Willie and Eddie.

Eddie complains of boredom to Willie as they kill time sitting with Aunt Lotte in the front room. Eva announces her plans to go to the movies, but when Lotte protests, she decides to ask Willie and Eddie to go along.

In the movie theater, Eddie comically sits between Eva and her date, who appears to be having less than a good time. When they drop the young man off at his house, Eva walks him to his door, provoking derision from the obviously smitten Eddie.

The next day, Eddie and Willie take a walk outside in the snow. Eddie is tired of Cleveland. "You know it's funny, you come to some place new," observes Eddie, "and everything looks just the same." "No kiddin', Eddie," Willie snorts derisively.

Eva confides to Willie that she wants to "get out" of Lotte's house in Cleveland. Willie tries to tell a joke, but fluffs it three times, giving up. "I can't remember this joke," he admits, "but it's good."

Lotte beats the two men at cards repeatedly, announcing "I am the veener." Eva gets a phone call from Billy, and she explains that she can't see him tonight because it is Willie and Eddie's last night in town. Eva invites the two to go look at the lake. "Go jump in the lake," says Lotte, obliviously.

The trio arrive at the lake and stand at a guard rail, buffeted by the howling wind. Gazing into the white void, Eva announces, "Well, this is it, Lake Erie." "It's beautiful," remarks Eddie, in typical deadpan fashion.

Back at Lotte's, Eva says goodbye to her friends. "So if you guys win a lot of money at the race track, you should try and kidnap me," says Eva. They drive off.

The plaintive music of a string quartet plays behind a title card: "Paradise."

Back in the car, Willie suggests taking a trip to Florida, and Eddie rhapsodizes about its virtues—white beaches, bikinis, flamingos. "You been there?" asks Willie. "No, I've never been there," he replies blankly. They decide to turn around and take Eva with them to "Paradise."

Eva is thrilled that they have returned for her, but Lotte loudly protests as she leaves. As they pull off, she mumbles to herself, "You son-of-a-bitch."

Eva pulls out her tape machine and plays the now-familiar "I Put a Spell on You," provoking the usual Willie response: "Not that, that's awful." "Screamin' Jay—he's my main man," Eva replies in a bland voice. "It's drivin' music," notes the approving Eddie.

The travelers press on, and eventually arrive at their destination. Stopping at a roadside business, they all don sunglasses. "Now we look like real tourists," observes Willie. They travel on to a beachside motel. Willie tells Eva to duck down in the backseat so that they can get away with paying for only two guests. Eva joins them in the room, and she and Willie each stretch out on a bed, leaving the folding cot for Eddie. Eddie wrestles with the cot in classic sit-com fashion. Eddie persuades Willie to go to the dog races tomorrow.

The next morning, Eva rises to find Willie and Eddie gone. Irritated at them for having abandoned her, she kills time waiting around for them. When they return, Eva chews them out for leaving her alone in a strange place, and they reveal that they have lost most of their money betting on dogs. Dejected, they walk on the windswept beach.

Back in the room, Willie paces nervously; he wants to try to win back their money at the horseraces. He refuses to allow Eva to join them, however, and dejected, she takes a walk alone.

Eva buys a wide-brimmed hat at roadside gift shop, donning it as she walks along the desolate oceanfront. A tall man approaches her and noting her hat, gives her a bulging envelope. Perplexed, Eva peeks inside the envelope and walks off. A few moments later, a tall lanky woman dressed in black and wearing a coincidentally similar wide-brimmed hat appears, searching in vain for her apparent connection.

Back at the motel, Eva closes the drapes and removes a large wad of currency from the envelope, leaving a portion of it along with a note for Willie and Eddie. Later, the two return drinking and singing, having apparently won back their money. They find the money and Willie reads Eva's note: she has gone to the airport to fly back to Hungary. They leave immediately to intercept her.

At the airport, Eva inquires about flights to Europe: the only flight remaining that day goes to Budapest. If she wants another European destination, she will have to wait until tomorrow. The flight to Budapest leaves in forty-four minutes, he tells her.

Willie and Eddie arrive at the airport later. Thinking Eva has boarded the Budapest flight, Willie buys a ticket so that he can board the airliner and take her off.

Outside, Eddie waits by the car. When a jet takes off and passes overhead, he assumes the worst, mumbling to himself, "Oh, Willy, I had a bad feeling. What the hell are you gonna do in Budapest?" He gets in the car and drives away.

Eva returns to their motel room, and plops herself in a chair before the window, holding the hat in her lap, looking off, her glance turned away from the view outside.

Stranger Than Paradise is one of the most strikingly original films to emerge in the 1980s. Tom DiCillo's work as cinematographer is particularly memorable.[10] The grim black-and-white photography manages to make the frigid Cleveland snowscapes look interchangable with sun-drenched Florida beaches, illustrating Eddie's droll observation, "You come to someplace new and everything looks just the same." The drab, diffuse lighting that pours through Willie's window from New York's slate-gray skies provides a fitting visual correlative to his featureless life. The influence of Ozu's static, tableau-like compositions are particularly evident in the film's interior scenes. No closeup shots break the flow of each master scene. An impassive witness to each scene, the camera stakes out a fixed position in each shot and, aside from an occasional pan or tilt to follow its subjects, seldom strays from its locked-down perch. But where Ozu's camera meets its characters at eye level, Jarmusch's camera often peers down at its characters, as if from the distant perspective of an uninvited visitor, left standing without a chair. Only occasionally, as in a scene when Willie and Eddie abscond with winnings from a poker game, does the camera offer an extreme high angle of the film's proceedings. The few moving camera shots appear to be taken from a rolling automobile, following along with the actors as they lope down the sidewalk. *Stranger Than Paradise* is especially notable for its use of negative space, in both its soundtrack and its photographic composition. The sound of characters shuffling their feet and fidgeting figures as prominently as their dialogue. The film's only music alternates between a lurching Screamin' Jay Hawkins blues wail and the bleak sounds of a Bartok-influenced string quartet.

Jarmusch may show us an ugly postindustrial world rife with pollution and garbage, but he peoples who world with characters that are sympathetic and humane. Despite the distancing effects of the film's mise-en-scène, the admittedly eccentric characters progressively ingratiate themselves upon the viewer through the course of the film's exposition. Always understated, Jarmusch's gentle, perceptive, and pervasive humor makes watching this otherwise bleak film a joyous experience. Aunt Lotte's protests at Eva's departure (topped by her only epithet, "you son-of-a-bitch"), Eva's even-toned and disarming defense of Screamin' Jay as her "main man," Willie's tongue-tied inability to tell a simple joke, and practically every amusing word that spouts from Eddie's mouth leaven what could otherwise be a rather flat and dreary film.

Stranger Than Paradise is typical of Jarmusch's elliptical narratives, similar in many respects to the novels of Kurt Vonnegut, Jr., who often ends popular books such as *Breakfast of Champions* with unorthodox last lines such as "so it goes" and "et cetera" to emphasize the goal-less odyssey each character continues after the book is finished:

> The story begins in the middle of their journeys. In the end, they continue. . . . The characters are always the center. I have to fall in love with them. . . . I can't even figuratively, at the end, have the curtain close and the story tied up, because, to me, that would be like killing them. "It's over; go home."[11]

After the success of *Stranger*, Jarmusch was inundated with scripts that he rejected out of hand because, as he explained in the *New York Times*, "They were mostly teenage sex comedies."[12] With a budget of $1 million from Island Pictures, Jarmusch made his second black-and-white feature, the "neo-beat-noir comedy" *Down by Law*, which met with mixed critical notices. His next film, the three-part *Mystery Train*, won an award for "best artistic contribution" at Cannes, but was also greeted with lukewarm notices by some critics. His *Night on Earth*, a picture in five segments that featured Winona Ryder and Gena Rowlands in small roles, dealt with humorous but unrelated taxi cab encounters occurring simultaneously one night in five corners of the earth.

Jarmusch, who also has directed music promos for the Talking Heads and Big Audio Dynamite, occasionally acts in bit roles in offbeat films himself. He continues to finance his feature films with foreign money—for example, *Mystery Train* was financed by the Japanese conglomerate JVC—and insists on owning the negatives of his films, giving him complete control over their distribution on video, television, and cable.

Jarmusch continues to make small films his way, essentially without Hollywood interference. He has refused to depict the usual Hollywood stereotypes motivated by greed, ambition, or sex, as he explained to David Sterritt of the *Christian Science Monitor*:

> Most people I know live in some way outside wage labor. They're artists, musicians, painters. I like characters who are on

the edge of things. I'm not really interested in characters who are motivated by careers or financial success. . . . I think all my films will be about marginal, outsider people.[13]

His refusal to go "commercial," along with his staunch independence and hip sense of aesthetics, has served as a model for a number of younger filmmakers, including Richard Linklater and Kevin Smith. His integrity intact, he is one of the few original independents to remain true to the American maverick spirit.

Thus Jarmusch, more so than any of the other independents, seems happy to eschew American commercial moviemaking, instead following in the art film tradition established by European filmmakers such as Chabrol, Godard, and Truffaut. Compared With his cult status in the United States, his mainstream success in Europe seems assured. By his own account, his follow-up to *Stranger Than Paradise,—Down by Law*—"made more money in its Paris run than in its entire release in the States."[14] Thus Jarmusch joins the ranks of other film mavericks, including Orson Welles and Robert Altman, who have had to count on the support of European *cineastes* to continue making their unique films.

NOTES

1. Jim Jarmusch, interview. Karen Schoemer, "Film as Life, and Vice Versa," *New York Times*, April 30, 1992, p. C1.

2. Jim Jarmusch, interview. Harlan Jacobson, "Three Guys in Three Directions; *Stranger Than Paradise*: $120,000," *Film Comment*, February 1985, p. 60.

3. Schoemer, "Film as Life," p. C1.

4. Jim Jarmusch, interview. Jane Shapiro, *Village Voice*, September 16, 1986, p. 49.

5. Jim Jarmusch, interview. Lawrence Van Gelder, *New York Times*, October 21, 1984, p. B4.

6. Ibid.

7. This thirty-minute film later screened at festivals as *The New World*, and became the first act of the finished *Stranger Than Paradise*.

8. *1990 Current Biography Yearbook*, p. 342.

9. Victoria Bugbee, "Stranger than Paradise," *American Cinematographer*, March 1985, p. 47.

10. Originally an actor, DiCillo later achieved success as an independent director in his own right with the largely Jarmusch-influenced *Johnny Suede* (1991) and the independent filmmaking satire *Living in Oblivion* (1995).

11. Jim Jarmusch, interview. Michael Wilmington, "Director Puts Much Value on Tough-Sell Reputation," *Los Angeles Times*, February 27, 1990, p. F2.

12. Maslin, p. B1.

13. Jim Jarmusch, interview. David Sterritt, *Christian Science Monitor*, October 4, 1984, p. 25.

14. Jim Jarmusch, interview. Lance Loud, "Jim Jarmusch Takes a Short-cut," *American Film*, January 1990, p. 16.

CHAPTER 6

Neon Noir:
Blood Simple
(1984)

USA: R

35mm Color

Running time: 97 minutes

Directed by Joel Coen

Cast in credits order:

   John Getz. . . . . Ray

   Frances McDormand. . . . . Abby

   Dan Hedaya. . . . . Julian Marty

   M. Emmet Walsh. . . . . Visser, a Private Detective

   Samm-Art Williams. . . . . Maurice

   Deborah Neumann. . . . . Debra

   Raquel Gavia. . . . . Landlady

   Van Brooks. . . . . Man from Lubbock

   William Creamer. . . . . Old Cracker

   Loren Bivens. . . . . Strip Bar Exhorter

   Bob McAdams. . . . . Strip Bar Senator

   Shannon Sedwick. . . . . Stripper

Nancy Finger. . . . . Girl on Overlook

Cinematography by Barry Sonnenfeld

Music by Carter Burwell

Written by

Ethan Coen

Joel Coen

Production design by Jane Musky

Costume design by Sara Medina-Pape

Edited by

Peggy Connolly

Roderick Jaynes

Don Wiegmann

> We were much more involved on a personal level with people who were making horror movies, exploitation movies, than we were with any sort of avant-garde New York art film scene or anything like that; we didn't know any of those people, whereas we knew people who were working on exploitation films.
>
> Joel Coen[1]

The same year Jim Jarmusch beguiled the art-film would with his deadpan comedy *Stranger Than Paradise*, another quirky yet entirely disparate vision was taking shape, this time from two sources working together as one: Joel and Ethan Coen. Their film *Blood Simple* put them on the map as one of the most intriguing and idiosyncratic partnerships to emerge in American film history.

The Coens' placid childhood in Midwest suburbia contrasts sharply with the menacing crime film that would make them famous. They were born, Joel in 1955 and Ethan in 1958, in St. Louis Park, Minnesota, a predominantly Jewish suburb of Minneapolis. Their parents were both academics, their father Edward a one-time University of Minnesota professor of economics and their mother Rena a professor of art history at St. Cloud State University. According to their mother, the two boys exhibited marked differences in temperament, with Joel "very social and gregarious" while Ethan "really very quiet, very reticent."[2] Despite their parents' scholarly pedigrees, the brothers admit to having very little high cultural upbringing, and instead spent much of their youth devouring B-movies on television: "We saw a lot of Tarzan movies and Steve Reeves muscle movies. . . . And we were into movies like *That Touch of Mink, A Global Affair*, Bob Hope movies, Jerry Lewis movies, anything with Tony Curtis, *Pillow Talk*. We tried to see everything with Doris Day. Those were important movies for us."[3]

Despite claims that their childhood and adolescence were uneventful and dull, the brothers forged a colorful partnership that would endure well into adulthood. Before they entered their teens, they launched a newsletter called *The Flag Avenue Sentinel* and sold it for two cents apiece to neighbors. The venture folded after two issues, but it was only a short time before Joel became interested in making films. With money earned mowing lawns, he bought a Super-8 movie camera, and before long he and Ethan were busy making their own B-movies, including remakes of Cornel Wilde pictures *Advise and Consent* and *The Naked Prey*—"bad Hollywood movies," Joel acknowledges, that "never should have been made in the first place."[4] They also made original films, with such titles as *Henry Kissinger—Man on the Go* and *Lumberjacks of the North*. The latter film prefigured the incongruous humor that would become a Coen trademark, as in one scene in which lumberjacks break for lunch and extract syrup-drenched pancakes from their coat and pants pockets.[5]

Joel left Minneapolis to attend Simon's Rock College in Massachusetts, and ultimately enrolled in film school at New York University. While he found film school uninspiring, he did make a number of shorts, among them his thirty-minute thesis, *Soundings* (about a woman who makes love to her deaf boyfriend while verbally fantasizing about a man in the next room), anticipating the offbeat sensibilities and warped humor of his later efforts.[6]

Joel spent a semester in the graduate film program at the University of Texas at Austin, then returned to New York to work as a production assistant for various documentary and industrial films. Barry Sonnenfeld— a cinematographer who later worked on several Coen pictures before becoming a director himself (*The Addams Family*)—hired Coen to work on some industrials, and remembers him as "the world's worst P.A. [production assistant]. He got three parking tickets, came late, set fire to the smoke machine."[7]

Despite his poor record as a P.A., Joel found work as an assistant editor on a number of low-budget horror films, including a cheapie called *Nightmare* (he was later fired) and two films by Sam Raimi: *Fear No Evil* and *The Evil Dead*. Joel found a longtime friend in Raimi and borrowed many of his highly mannered cinematic techniques: accelerated ground-level tracking shots, swooping camera moves, and restless souped-up POV shots adapted from Hitchcock films. The most interesting devices to find their way into the Coen's book of cut-rate camera tricks were the "shakycam," a camera mounted to an eight-foot stud carried by two grips, and the "blankycam," a camera and operator dragged on a blanket across a smooth floor. These types of shots became a key part of the Coen visual vocabulary. They figure prominently in *Blood Simple* and reappear in the Coens' later films.[8]

In the meantime, Ethan had received his degree in philosophy at Princeton. He joined his brother in New York, and together they turned out several scripts, including a screwball comedy entitled *Coast to Coast*, centered on a Red Chinese plot to produce multiple clones of Albert Einstein. They also collaborated with Raimi on a script they called *The XYZ Murders*, a story about two rat exterminators hired to commit a murder. Raimi later directed the film in 1985; all three ultimately disavowed the finished product (retitled *Crimewave*), claiming that the original concept was butchered by the distributor.

The pair began writing a story set in the barren hills and smoky roadhouses Joel Coen knew in Austin. The brothers then found an attorney who helped them set up a limited partnership for a feature film venture and they returned to Minneapolis to scare up investors. To raise money, they made a short 35mm "preview of coming attractions" reel—depicting shots of hands loading a gun, a man being buried alive, and shafts of light streaming through bullet holes in a wall—all promoting a film that had yet to be made. Finding that few could attend their screenings, the Coens lugged a projector and a 16mm reduction print around to prospective investors' homes and workplaces. Joel found the trailer instrumental for raising money through a Jewish philanthropic organization, and armed "with a list of the hundred richest Jews in town," Sonnenfeld raised $750,000 in nine months.[9]

Ethan and Joel wrote the script for *Blood Simple* in 1980, working on weekends and evenings. Although the brothers cut their cinematic teeth watching B-movies, *Blood Simple* (which derives its title from a line in Dashiell Hammett's pulp novel *Red Harvest*)[10] derives from their love for literary pulp fiction, particularly the works of James M. Cain. They bypassed film versions of Cain's stories, including *The Postman Always Rings Twice* and *Double Indemnity*, and went directly to the source—the novels—for inspiration. As Joel noted later, "We liked his hard-boiled style and wanted to write a James M. Cain story and put it in a modern context."

The film opens with scenes of desolate oil fields behind the slurred words of an ominous voiceover: "The world is full of complainers. The fact is, nothin' comes with a guarantee. And I don't care if you're the Pope of Rome, the President of the United States, or Man of the Year. Something can all go wrong."

A man and a woman are driving on a rainy night. Their conversation tells the viewer that they are illicit lovers: she is married to his employer. The woman, Abby, orders him to stop the car. A Volkswagen beetle appears to have been following them. The bug turns around and drives off. "What do you want to do?" he asks. "What do you want to do?" she asks back.

The answer arrives in the next scene, as the couple make love in a motel room. In the morning a telephone call rouses the two; on the other end a mysterious voice asks, "Are you havin' a good time?" The woman asks who it is, the man, Ray, replies "your husband."

In a roadhouse, Visser, a sleazy detective dressed in a pale-yellow leisure suit sits down with bar owner Julian Marty, showing him some compromising 8 x10s of his wife in bed with her lover. Marty, disgusted at the news, throws an envelope stuffed with currency at Visser's feet. "It ain't such bad news," the sleuth mumbles, "You thought he was colored." Visser shuffles out. Out on the main floor, the black bartender Maurice reminds a patron that it is "Yankee Night" and selects a cover of a Monkees hit on the jukebox. Marty approaches the bar and attempts to pick up an attractive blonde, who professes to be a longtime friend of the bartender. Marty slinks away when Maurice returns to the bar and asks the woman, "What'd you say your last name was?"

A mobile camera follows a German Shepherd down the hallway of Marty's palatial house, where Ray shoots pool and gazes at family portraits while he waits for Abby. Ray tells her he'll drop her at a motel and make a last trip to the bar "to see a guy."

At the roadhouse, an unmotivated floating camera takes us down the length of the bar, hopping over a passed-out drunk, as Ray approaches Maurice and the blonde woman. He goes out to ask Marty for his past two weeks' salary, while Marty denigrates Abby and threatens Ray. "Come on this property again and I'll be forced to shoot you." He calls Abby from his office, but hangs up without speaking.

Ray comes home as Abby hangs up the phone, and he is suspicious about her after having heard Ray's admonitions. "You want the bed or the couch?" he asks. She takes the couch, restlessly watching the turning of an overhead fan. She rises and walks gingerly down the hall to Ray, whom she joins in bed. The next morning, Abby finds herself alone and stands in her nightgown looking at her reflection in a compact case. When she notices Marty's dog in the house, she knows something is wrong. Suddenly Marty grabs her from behind, dragging her outside. A furiously charging shakycam sails across the lawn and up the struggling man and woman as Abby ends his attack with bitten finger and a well-placed kick to the groin. Marty slinks off and drives away as Ray emerges from the house and takes the startled woman in his arms.

One day Marty meets Visser at a secluded teen hangout overlooking a river, and offers him $10,000 to kill Abby and Ray. Visser agrees and tells him to go to "Corpus" for a few days, to "get hisself noticed." Marty tells him to dispose of the bodies in the big incinerator.

A Latino woman shows Abby a loft to let, shouting at a man who sits inside on a bench. Back at the roadhouse, Abby asks Maurice to keep an eye on Ray and Marty; he tells her Marty has gone to Corpus.

In bed with Ray, Abby can't sleep. Outside we see the ominous Volkswagen. A creeping POV takes us through the living room of the flat to the front doorknob, as Visser cracks the door and enters. He rifles her purse, removes a revolver, and tiptoes to their bedroom door. After hearing a noise, he heads back outside and around to the window of the sleeping couple. A flash.

The next day, Visser calls Marty, telling him the deed has been accomplished. That night after the roadhouse has closed, he shows Marty some photographs of the couple in apparently bloodstained sheets. Marty becomes nauseated and goes to the restroom to throw up. Marty returns and extracts a wad of bills from the tavern safe, leaving a folded envelope inside. "We need to learn to be discreet. Trust each other," he coolly observes, and slides the money and photos back across the desk. Visser produces the revolver and shoots Marty in the chest. Kicking the gun away, Visser takes the money. A high-angle shot pulls directly over the dead man as the blades of the barely turning fan move across the frame.

Ray enters the empty roadhouse, looking for his money. He knocks on the office door and enters, calling out to Marty. As Ray approaches the lifeless figure, a gun goes off and slides down the floor, startling Ray. He picks up the gun: it's Abby's pearl-handled revolver. He surveys Marty's bleeding body and places the gun on the desk. Someone knocks on the door, startling Ray; it's Maurice, who has brought a woman back to the tavern, "It's Ladies Night," he says. Ray, nervous that the murder might be linked to him, frantically mops up blood, takes the gun, and drags the corpse out to his car.

Throwing Marty's body in the back of the car, he drives over to the incinerator, passing it by and continuing down the road. Hearing a murmur from the body, Ray quickly pulls over beside a dirt field and runs furiously, stops, and returns. As he reaches the far side of the car, he sees that Marty is alive and crawling down the road. Ray pulls the car back, stares in disbelief, and pulls a shovel out of the back. He walks up to Marty and prepares to brain him, when a truck appears on the horizon. Ray quickly pulls Marty from the road as the semi roars by. He digs a shallow grave among the furrows, throwing in Marty. As he tosses shovelfuls of dirt on the dying man, Marty pulls the revolver, but cannot shoot. Ray finishes burying him, and as day breaks he drives away. He calls Abby from a gas station, and goes home to her.

In a darkroom, Visser burns the photos of the sleeping couple, we see to have been retouched to simulate bloody corpses. He is unpleasantly surprised to learn he has forgotten his lighter at the tavern.

Meanwhile, Ray can't sleep; he speaks in broken sentences to Abby, who can't understand his paranoia. "Where the hell's my windbreaker?" he wonders. The phone rings, but the caller hangs up when she answers. "It's Marty," she supposes. Ray walks out, leaving her pistol on a table by the door.

Maurice checks his telephone answering machine and hears a message from the night before: Marty claims that money is missing from the safe. His hand comes down to shut off the machine, dissolving to Ray's finger descending to touch a spot of blood staining his backseat. Maurice pulls up to confront Ray with the news. "You shouldn't have taken the fuckin' money," he says, and drives away. Meanwhile the blood seeps through the towel Ray has thrown over the seat.

Abby pulls up before the roadhouse as Visser beats something inside the office. He hides when Abby enters, spying on her as she discovers a towel-wrapped hammer and damage done to the safe. The fish stare at her in silence.

Her head falls onto her pillow back in bed at her loft. Sleepless, she throws water on her face in the bathroom, and hears a strange noise. It's Marty, sitting on her bed. "I love you. That's a stupid thing to say, right?" he says. Suddenly, he spits up a profusion of blood. Abby sits up in bed, awakening from a nightmare.

Abby pulls up at Ray's; he's packed all his belongings in boxes. Ray confesses his live burial of Marty, punctuated as a flying newspaper hits the screendoor with a crash. Abby rushes over to get some answers from Maurice, who insists that Marty is still alive; nonetheless, he warns her to "stay away from Ray. The guy's gone nuts."

Ray noses around the roadhouse, finding one of the doctored photographs. He gets into his car, the ominous VW beetle waiting behind.

Back at Abby's loft, Ray stares nervously out the window, and is felled by a shot from outside. Abby dives to the floor and puts out the lamp with a thrown shoe. Footsteps outside the door preface the turning of the front door bolt as Visser opens the door and enters. Abby hides in the bathroom while he pats Ray's body, looking for the money.

Visser enters the bathroom, searching for the woman, who has crept outside the window and into the next room. He reaches around to the next window, only to have a knife slam down, pinning his hand to the sill. Gunshots ring out as bullets blast holes through the wall, allowing shafts of light to pour through. Visser's fist bursts through the plaster, and pulls the blade from the impaled other hand. As he creeps to the door, Abby, almost reluctantly, palms her revolver and shoots the sleuth through the door, to the end mistaking him for someone else (in this case Marty). Visser dies on the floor, but not until he has the last joking word: "Well, ma'am, if I see him, I'll sure give him the message." The film ends from the dying man's POV, as a water droplet poises to drip from a knot of undersink plumbing.

Despite the Coens' professed unfamiliarity with art films, they based much of *Blood Simple*'s photographic style on Vittorio Storaro's vivid cinematography for Bernardo Bertolucci's seminal *The Conformist*. Cinematographer Barry Sonnenfeld was also influenced by Robby Müller's haunting imagery for Wim Wenders' *The American Friend*. In a similar vein, *Blood Simple* 's generous use of chartreuse, salmon, and magenta gels evokes the acid illumination of neon and sodium lamps. The predominantly unnatural color scheme deprives the images of solidity; in this respect the Coens' film departs from the classic *noir* films that sculpted their subjects in a black-and-white bas-relief of light and shadow.

Blood Simple trots out tried-and-true film noir themes of adultery and treachery along with their attendant fetishistic visual motifs, but ultimately betrays a closer kinship with the "mad slasher" genre than with any detective film. Raimi identified the formula and basic premise of *Blood Simple* as one shared in their early films: "The innocent must suffer; the guilty must be punished; you must taste blood to be a man," and "the dead must walk." Indeed, the restless dolly and shakycam shots recall the *Halloween*-inspired stalker POVs that defined low-budget horror movies of the seventies and eighties. These shots placed the viewer in visual empathy with an unearthly or supernatural being that prowls over lawns and through houses, watching proceedings unfold and lying in wait for deluded characters to trip up in their misguided machinations. The Coens' techniques, if self-conscious and contrived, are nonetheless often highly inventive and imaginative, and they are often downright hilarious.

Many reviewers praised the performances in *Blood Simple*, but closer inspection reveals acting that is mostly stiff and unnecessarily mannered. The performers navigate the narrative obstacle course like so many balls bouncing numbly off the bumpers of a malevolent pinball machine. John Getz's Ray broods vacuously through most of the film's twists and turns, face frozen in a lugubrious gaze, while Frances McDormand's constant reaction is a blank, wide-eyed gape, evoking a drugged Hayley Mills. For a purportedly lurid, sex-driven tale, it is difficult to feel any convincing sexual chemistry (or even a smolder) between Ray and Abby, an absolute requisite for Cain-style intrigue and adultery. Hence, there are no scenes of unbridled passion here, aside from a brief shot of the lovers awkwardly bumping about in a motel bed. M. Emmet Walsh is a cloying, word-slurring stereotype of a divorce detective, a cross between Orson Welles's Hank Quinlan (the corrupt sheriff of *Touch of Evil*) and the demented turkey hunter from Errol Morris's *Vernon, Florida*. And Dan Hedaya's dyspeptic Marty, an incongruous Richard Nixon lookalike, is laughably both tense and terse in his reactions to the malignant events swirling around him.

The film churns with crime film allusions and standard genre fetishes— the languid rotations of overhead fans, putrefying catfish symbolizing the completion of a hit, a pearl-handled revolver, the monogrammed Zippo lighter (inscribed "Man of the Year") carelessly left at the scene of the crime. Ray shows some of the same droll irreverence (but none of the irreverent wit) for statuary that Dick Powell did in *Murder My Sweet*, tucking his cigarette into the mouth of a stuffed peccary in Marty's game room.

Critics waxed enthusiastic about the movie. David Denby of *New York* magazine lauded it as "the most brazenly self-assured directorial debut in American film history," with "enough humor to prevent [the] material from turning into crude, primal pulp. . . . Together, the Coens concocted a plot rich in surprise, betrayal, and coincidence—a thoroughly satisfying old-fashioned tale."[11] Others who saw more flamboyant style than substance were not impressed. Pauline Kael of *The New Yorker* dryly noted that "the reason the camera whoop-de-do is so noticeable is that there's nothing else going on."[12]

Many resented the rush to praise *Blood Simple* as a work of art. Kenneth Geist of *Films in Review* wrote "Had it not been for the lavish critical reception *Blood Simple* received at last fall's N.Y. Film festival, the film might well have vanished. Critical puffery, however, has made this little shocker into a fashionable art house attraction."[13] Another dismissed it as having "the heart of a Bloomingdale's window and the soul of a resume."[14] Still, one critic spoke for many of the film's fans when he praised "the Coen's camera" as "a participant in the action, and worlds hipper than anyone on-screen. 'Hi, I'm here,' it as much as says, 'and I'm *soooo* smart.' "[15]

There is something fundamentally annoying about *Blood Simple* that irritates in an incipient, barely perceptible fashion—like the pesky fly that crawls around M. Emmet Walsh's ear and temple. Garish and vacuous, *Blood Simple* is, in the final analysis, a catalogue of noir and suspense clichés, a film about unpleasant characters that is itself unpleasant to watch. In a revealing comment, Ethan Coen summed it up best: "I saw *Blood Simple* on TV a while ago, and I enjoyed it because it . . . had commercials. If you had hooked my brain up with electrodes, you'd have seen a big spike of interest when the Ty-D-Bol man came on."[16]

After the success of *Blood Simple*, Joel and Ethan Coen's futures were secure. They went on to write, direct, and produce many strikingly different features, crossing genre lines and serving up more of the trademark Coen wit. On the heels of *Blood Simple* came the Coens' most successful film, *Raising Arizona*—a manic, surreal tale of a petty criminal who kidnaps an infant to satisfy his barren former police officer wife, and the improbable consequences that follow. Produced for a mere $6 million, *Raising Arizona* pulled more than $22 million at the box office.

Next, the brothers revisited the hard-boiled film noir genre for *Miller's Crossing*, focusing on a violent power struggle between the Irish and Italian factions of a Louisiana town in the 1920s. Critical reaction was even more mixed than with earlier films. While one reviewer called it "the best picture yet from the Coen brothers,"[17] another complained that the picture had "no life of its own, and the Coens' formal control and meticulously crafted ironies become, after a while, rather depressing."[18]

While writing *Miller's Crossing*, the brothers found that even the writer's block they suffered could become a story, and in three weeks turned out the script for *Barton Fink*, about a pompous Clifford Odets–inspired playwright lured to 1930s Hollywood to write a "Wallace Beery wrestling picture." Critics predictably split on the picture, although one pundit observed that the filmmakers had "redeemed the emptiness in their earlier work by taking emptiness itself as a subject."[19] The picture was an unprecedented success at the Cannes Film Festival, becoming the first film in the exposition's history to win three major awards—the Palme d'Or for best film, and prizes for best director and best actor.

The Hudsucker Proxy, Joel and Ethan's most lavish and expensive project to date, was financed at over $40 million. This time the script, written with longtime collaborator and friend Sam Raimi, centered on a naïve employee's ascent through the ranks of a huge novelty manufacturing business. He becomes the improbable president of the firm as a pawn in a villainous executive's plan to devalue the company's stock.

Veteran Hollywood producer Joel Silver, impressed by the success accorded *Blood Simple*, agreed to produce the film, despite the fact that *Barton Fink* made less than $5 million on a $9 million production cost. The action film mogul was taken aback, however, when the brothers threatened to pull out of the project when the studio insisted they cast a star, Paul Newman, in a major role. Alarmed at the worst-case scenario that *Proxy* might be "perceived as a *festival film*," Silver warned the brothers that "if they intend to continue making mainstream, higher-budget films, this film is going to have to deliver asses on seats."[20] Newman was ultimately cast as the film's antagonist, but Silver's trepidations proved to be an omen as more critics than ever panned the Coens and their film, citing now-familiar complaints of heartlessness and slavish adherence to artifice at the expense of story and character. Unfazed, they began production on their next project, *Fargo*, in January 1995.

The Coens continue to assert creative control over their projects, despite their increasing involvement with Hollywood. While the films they create are often seen as coldly manipulative and obsessed with ostentatious visual and cinematic display for its own sake, their works are often saved by the richness and craft of their writing. They have demonstrated their gifts for writing witty dialogue, revitalizing time-worn genres with unpredictable plot twists, and ability to create full-color, three-dimensional fantasy worlds peopled with vivid and delightfully quirky characters. If they can coalesce their staunch independence without caving in to the fiduciary demands of the motion picture industry, their career promises many more interesting and diverse projects for the future.

NOTES

1. Joel Coen, interview. "Views from the Edge," *American Cinema*, Public Broadcasting System, KCET, Los Angeles, April 30, 1995.

2. Joel Coen, interview, *Entertainment Weekly*, February 28, 1992, p. 9.

3. Ibid., p. 2.

4. Joel and Ethan Coen, interview. Hal Hinson, "Bloodlines," *Film Comment*, March-April 1985, p. 14.

5. *Current Biography Yearbook* (1994) p. 117.

6. Ibid.

7. Eric Pooley, "Warped in America: The Dark Vision of Moviemakers Joel and Ethan Coen," *New York*, March 23, 1987, p. 44.

8. Mark Horowitz, "Coen Brothers A-Z: The Big Two-Headed Picture," *Film Comment*, September-October 1991, p. 43.

9. Pooley, "Warped in America," p. 48.

10. The term refers to a muddled state of mind which supposedly occurs in a killer's mind after committing a murder.

11. David Denby, *New York*, January 21, 1985, p. 51.

12. Pauline Kael, *New Yorker*, February 25, 1985, p. 81.

13. Kenneth Geist, *Films in Review*, May 1985, p. 304.

14. J. Hoberman, *The Village Voice*, January 22, 1985, p. 53.

15. Richard Corliss, *Time*, January 28, 1985.

16. Tad Friend, "Inside the Coen Heads." *Vogue*, April 1994, p. 408.

17. Peter Travers, *Rolling Stone*, October 4, 1990.

18. Terrence Rafferty, *The New Yorker*, October 29, 1990, p. 39.

19. Dave Kehr, *Chicago Tribune*, August 23, 1991, p. C1.

20. Joel Silver, interview. *Vogue*, April 1994, p. 407.

CHAPTER 7

Brooklyn Broach:
She's Gotta Have It
(1986)

USA: R

Super 16mm Black and White

Running time: 84 minutes

Directed by Spike Lee

Cast in alphabetical order:

Cheryl Burr. . . . . Ava

Raye Dowell. . . . . Opal Gilstrap

Aaron Dugger. . . . . Noble

Tommy Redmond Hicks. . . . . Jamie Overstreet

Tracy Camilla Johns. . . . . Nola Darling

Bill Lee. . . . . Sonny Darling

Joie Lee. . . . . Clorinda Bradford

Spike Lee. . . . . Mars Blackmon

Epatha Merkinson. . . . . Doctor Jamison

John Canada Terrell. . . . . Greer Childs

Cinematography by Ernest Dickerson

Music by Bill Lee

Written by Spike Lee
Production designed by Wynn Thomas
Costume design by John Michael Reefer
Edited by Spike Lee
Produced by Shelton J. Lee

> In the history of American cinema, too, too often black people
> have had to rely on Hollywood to tell our stories. I'm deter-
> mined to change that even if it's in only a small way. We
> shouldn't have to rely on the Spielbergs[1] to define our existence.
> Blacks have to produce their own films, period."
>
> Spike Lee[2]

The first black filmmaker to enjoy major success since the "Black film"
renaissance of the early 1970s, Spike Lee has managed to create his own
niche while spawning an entire black filmmaking movement. Perhaps the
most celebrated black filmmaker in motion picture history, he has exerted
an incalculable influence on American filmmaking in general, opening
doors for John Singleton, Matty Rich, Mario Van Peebles, the Hudlin
brothers, Ernest Dickerson, and Robert Townshend, among others.

Lee has earned himself a reputation for lambasting the racial prejudices
of white America with such films as *Do the Right Thing* and *Malcolm X*, but
the film that launched his career was his first feature, *She's Gotta Have It*, an
audacious, confident seriocomedy that unapologetically broached the subject of female sexual freedom in its story of a woman who juggles three
lovers, told from the perspective of each character.

The son of renowned jazz double-bassist Bill Lee, Shelton Jackson Lee
was born in 1957 in Atlanta, Georgia. The nickname "Spike" was bestowed
upon him by his mother, Jacquelyn, shortly after his birth. He and his family
lived in Chicago briefly before settling down in the middle-class Fort
Greene neighborhood of Brooklyn. During much of Lee's childhood, the
family lived on the earnings of his mother, a high school teacher, as his
father's reluctance to adopt the increasingly popular electric bass restricted
his ability to find work.

Lee attended Morehouse College in Atlanta (as did his grandfather and
father), where he graduated in 1979. Those years made a profound and
lasting impression on Lee, where he enjoyed "the wonderful feeling . . .
where everybody is black,"[3] which he documented in his later feature *School
Daze*. Majoring in mass communications, Lee was an outgoing student and
worked as a writer for the school paper, acted as a disc jockey for a local
radio station, and directed the lavish Morehouse homecoming coronation
pageant in his senior year.

Lee developed an interest in film in his sophomore year, purchasing his first Super-8 camera. He made a number of small films, including *The Talented Tenth*, self-described as "a corny love story at a black campus,"[4] and several "dance pieces," including *Last Hustle in Brooklyn*, which mixed disco music with scenes of the 1977 New York blackout.

After his graduation, Lee worked for a time as an intern at Columbia Pictures in Burbank, California. He returned to New York to enroll as a graduate in the Institute of Film and Television of New York University's Tisch School of the Arts. He didn't want to attend a Southern California film school, largely because he "couldn't drive" a car, and was anxious to return to his home of New York, where he felt he more easily could establish professional ties. The first years at NYU were frustrating for Lee, one of the few blacks at the school. His student film *The Answer* met with faculty disapproval, dealing as it did with "a black screenwriter hired to direct a fifty-million dollar remake of *Birth of a Nation*," which dared to "denigrate the father of cinema, D. W. Griffith."[5] Lee claimed he was nearly dismissed for his alleged failure to grasp "film grammar," but he was nevertheless granted a teaching assistantship that enabled him to work in the film equipment room in exchange for full tuition.[6] This allowed him to devote money given him by his grandmother to the funding of his films. His next film, *Sarah*, about Thanksgiving with a Harlem family, marked the beginning of his long and fruitful association with cinematographer Ernest Dickerson, who would shoot several of Lee's most important films.

Lee collaborated with Dickerson in their final year at NYU on Lee's master film thesis, *Joe's Bed-Stuy Barbershop: We Cut Heads*. With a score by Bill Lee, *Barbershop* featured Lee's longtime friend and co-producer Monty Ross as a Brooklyn ghetto barber who opens his shop to an illegal numbers racket in order to augment his meager income. The film brought Lee recognition as a serious filmmaker, earning him a Student Academy Award. It became the first student film to win a slot in Lincoln Center's prestigious New Directors/New Films series, where it met with mostly warm critical notices. The student film went on to a successful run at film festivals in San Francisco, Los Angeles, Atlanta, and Locarno, Switzerland.

Lee completed his masters degree in 1982, and on the basis of *Barbershop*'s success, was signed by the ICM and William Morris talent agencies. Representation brought no offers of employment in the film industry, however, which did not surprise the cynical Lee: "That cemented in my mind what I always thought all along, that I would have to go out and do it alone, not rely on anyone else."[7] He determined to produce and direct his own movies all the while working for $200 a week cleaning and shipping film for a local distribution house.

Two years after completing *Barbershop*, Lee was awarded a grant to make a film entitled *Messenger*, about a New York bicycle courier and his family. After running up expenses in excess of $40,000, the ill-fated film stalled and died after eight weeks of preproduction when the Screen Actors Guild cited the film as being "too commercial" and refused to grant him a low-budget waiver of its high union wages. Lee, in what would be one of many denunciations of perceived prejudice, called the debacle "a definite case of racism."[8]

Lee wasted little time in moving on to a new project, "a movie that would have very few characters, and needed next to no location work, sets, or costumes."[9] To help him write a story about a sexually liberated woman, Lee sought the help of friend Tracey Willard and compiled a forty-question "Advanced Sexual Syndrome Survey," conducting interviews with some thirty-two women to research his new idea. Unable to afford a typewriter, he hand-wrote the script for what would be his first feature film, *She's Gotta Have It*, the story of Nola Darling, an independent woman who tries to balance simultaneous relationships with three lovers of wildly disparate personalities. Patching together funding from several grants (he encountered resistance from one organization on the basis of the film's "sexist" content, and was denied a previously approved grant from AFI), Lee shot the film in Super 16mm[10] over twelve days in the summer of 1985, on a production budget of only $22,000.

Lee's all-black cast of hip, urbane, and dignified characters broke with established Hollywood stereotypes.[11] Thus, Lee correctly predicted that the film would find success in Europe:[12] "On a whole they are fascinated by blacks, anything American stuff. And they had never seen black people portrayed like this in a movie."[13] After the film drew raves in Cannes, Lee decided to forgo the New York Film Festival (held in October) and open the film in August: "There's a time period in August where, film-wise, everything is dead. All the summer films have died by then and so if you have something good it will take off."[14] *She's Gotta Have It* was the first by an independent black filmmaker to receive major distribution since Melvin Van Peebles's *Sweet Sweetback's Baadasss Song* in 1971. It kicked off a bidding war that pitted Island Pictures against Goldwyn; the former prevailed, offering Lee $450,000 for the negative pickup. The film, completed at a cost of $175,000, would ultimately gross over $8.5 million, nearly 25 precent of it in its first three weeks of release.

The film begins with melancholy piano music and a quote from Zora Neale Hurston, followed by opening credits and a montage of stills illustrating various informal portraits and Brooklyn street scenes. A dolly shot rolls into the bedroom-loft of protagonist Nola Darling. Sitting on a platform bed bedecked with candles, Nola directly addresses the viewer in a characteristic technique used throughout the film. The film alternates in tone from the omniscient perspective of a straight dramatic film to a confessional pseudo-documentary style, with Nola (and others) speaking as if to an interviewer conducting a study. She begins, "I want you to know the only reason I'm consenting to this is because I wish to clear my name." Apparently, some consider her a promiscuous "freak."

On a park bench, Nola's sensitive and soft-spoken lover Jamie Overstreet rhapsodizes about his "true" love. "Do you really mean that?" Nola asks him by the glimmering candlelight of her bedroom. Jamie, having suddenly appeared beside Nola, assures her and they make love, writhing silhouettes in the half-light of the loft. The lovers enjoy the afterglow, as Nola tells Jamie that she can make love only in her own "loving bed."

Next, Nola's former roommate Clorinda Bradford is introduced. Nola and she had "a big falling out" over Nola's unending amorous activities in the apartment. Fed up, Clorinda moved out, though she and Nola are still friends.

Nola speaks to the camera about her negative experiences with men, illustrated by a montage of "dogs": some twenty-odd men each photographed separately in black limbo shots, reciting various come-ons ranging from the banal to the ludicrous. Nola acknowledges that one was different, and a series of "stolen shots" provides a flashback to the time when she and Jamie first met in a busy Brooklyn street.

The sound of hip-hop music, film crew laughter,[15] and the image of a bicyclist careening headlong into the camera announces the arrival of Lover number 2, Mars Blackmon (played by Lee himself). Decked out in cap, gold name medallion and belt buckle, and Nike shoes, the bug-eyed Mars peers into the camera's wide-angle lens and testifies: "Nola had the goods and she knew what to do. All men want freaks—we just don't want 'em for a wife." He carries his bike up to her loft, where he and Nola flirt playfully in a languorous long take.

Back on his park bench, Jamie worries aloud about a woman he thinks has designs on Nola. That woman, Opal Gilstrap, now speaks to the camera from the stoop of a brownstone. She wants Nola to "be open-minded" about lesbianism. In Nola's flat, Opal fixes her a cup of tea and speaks the praises of her own sexual lifestyle. Jamie arrives and, sensing her intentions, becomes jealous and tells her to leave. Jamie grills Nola about her relationship with Opal, but she insists they are only friends.

Lover number 3, pretty boy Greer Childs, drives on-screen in a Jaguar XKE. A ludicrously stereotypical narcissist with gassed-back hair, he mouths lines such as "I was the best thing that ever happened to Nola Darling." He does pushups while preaching the benefits of exercise to Nola. An apparent obsessive-compulsive personality type, Greer spends so much time neatly folding and hanging his clothes that Nola falls asleep with boredom waiting for her beau to make love to her. The sex they do have, however, is varied and long-lasting, shot imaginatively as a montage of positions from a bird's-eye view of the bed to the rhythmic backdrop of a primal drumbeat.[16]

On Nola's birthday, Jamie prepares a special surprise. He tells her she must first close her eyes, click her heels three times, and repeat the familiar chant from *The Wizard of Oz*: "There's no place like home." In the tradition of the famous children's film, the black-and-white photography magically gives way to a fantasy shot in vivid primary colors, wherein the couple meet in a park to watch a dramatic dance sequence that Jamie has choreographed. The stage is a graffiti-scarred monument festooned with balloons and a large banner: "Happy Birthday Nola." The piece ends, and the two dancers present Nola with a cake topped by a single candle.[17]

Later, Jamie and Nola loll in bed, but their idyll is disturbed by a phone call from Mars. Jamie hands the phone to Nola; on the other end, Mars pleads for sex in his droll patter: "Please, baby, please, baby, please, baby, baby, please." Nola refuses him, but Jamie is clearly miffed.

Again at his commentator's perch on the park bench, Jamie recites a sappy poem he has composed. Nola continues the poem, as Jamie lies beside her in bed. Leaning confidentially over his bicycle handlebars, Mars cuts in to guffaw, "That's the worst piece of shit I ever heard, and Nola fell for it."

The "world-famous slow-motion Mt. Kilimanjaro nipple shot"[18] follows, as Mars kisses Nola's breast and licks her navel, and she shivers with glee. We hear a voiceover from Mars protesting "Stop!" as Nola lightly brushes her foot down the naked legs of Mars, sneakers still on his feet. Waking beside Nola, Mars professes his love for her, something she doesn't want to hear. He pulls Nola's panties over his head in a strained display of spontaneity and humor, and she in turn "greases" his scalp for him, a sensation he verifies as "better than bonin'." While Nola and Mars cavort, Jamie calls, but Mars kicks the phone to the floor. Jamie's angry retort from his philosopher's bench about being a mere "spoke in a wheel" reveals his conviction that for Nola, lovers are practically interchangable. He warns: "One day you're gonna wake up in this bed, and I'm gonna be long gone."

Greer appears on the scene again. He lectures to Nola as they stroll through a garden, calling her a "sex addict" and advising her to get professional help.

A handheld point-of-view shot leads past a receptionist and into the office of Dr. Jamison, who addresses the camera with an accounting of Nola's visit. In a therapy session, Nola refutes Greer's assertion that she is a sex addict. The counselor agrees and tells her not to "confuse a healthy sex drive with a sickness." The counselor again addresses the camera to verify that Nola is indeed "a healthy human being."

(This odd scene may have been included to reassure the audience that Lee does not wish them to see Nola merely as an oversexed trollop. Its inclusion may have been prompted by his fears of being labeled sexist, in light of the grant troubles he endured in preproduction. Its apologetic, politically correct tone sets it apart from the rest of the film.)

From his rowing machine, Greer protests the findings of the therapist. Nola, from her bed, laughs "he couldn't handle it, he got turned out."

A photo montage depicts the coming of winter in Fort Greene Park outside Nola's flat. A closeup of Jamie saying grace indicates that Thanksgiving has arrived. As he finishes the prayer, a chorus of "Amens" reveal that all three lovers have been invited to share Thanksgiving dinner with Nola, a plentitude of bounty indeed. Haughty Greer and squirrely Mars bicker throughout dinner; Greer leaves the table, followed by Nola. In an aside to Jamie, Mars offers to split their time weekly with Nola, tipping the balance of four days to Jamie. "But I get weekends, though," insists Mars.

Over a game of Scrabble, the men break into further arguments. Nola, disgusted, abandons her guests and retires to bed. A high-angle shot reveals Jamie and Nola lying side-by-side some time later, while Greer sits off in a chair and Mars slouches across the foot of the bed. Greer finally gives up and leaves, followed by Mars.

Nola's thoughts are played out in a dream sequence in which three women burst into the room and accuse Nola of stealing their men. One woman thrusts a lit match toward her, threatening to set her on fire. An image of flames is followed by two shots of Nola doubling up in bed. She screams "Fire!" aloud, waking Jamie. She and Jamie then argue over her desire to see Mars again. Jamie gives her an ultimatum: If she doesn't drop her lovers he will have nothing more to do with her.

Jamie's admonitions go unheeded as a bird's-eye shot shows Greer and Nola sunbathing on a rooftop, heads opposed. Greer tries to persuade her to vacation with him and date him exclusively.

From his familiar park bench, Jamie tries to confide to the camera when Mars abruptly rides up on his bicycle. Mars complains that Nola stood him up for a date: "That girl's as dependable as a ripped diaphragm." A passing skirt stops the conversation, and when they stop gawking, they return to talking about Nola. Mars leaves.

In Nola's kitchen Jamie tries to persuade Nola to love him alone; he only becomes frustrated and angry. Leaving, he passes Opal Gilstrap on her way up to visit. Opal sits down on the bed with Nola and kisses her, but Nola rebuffs further advances. After Opal leaves, Nola lies on the bed and silently touches herself. Frustrated, she calls Jamie later that night. He is in bed with another woman, but Nola begs him to come be with her; she says she needs him.

A still-photograph montage depicts Jamie's subway journey to the flat. "I knew you'd come if I asked," she admits, which only angers Jamie. She tries to kiss him deeply, but he resists.

> **NOLA:** Make love to me.
>
> **JAMIE:** You don't want me to make love to you. You want me to fuck you.

Jamie pulls her over to the bed and forces her down, taking her violently from behind. "Is this the way you like it? Does Greer do it like this? Does Mars?" Jamie shouts as he thrusts into her repeatedly; the form of Greer, then Mars takes his place in a sequence of expressionistic editing. Disgusted with Nola and himself, he admits before leaving her loft: "Here I'm trying to dog you the best I can, and what bothers me is I enjoyed it." Nola bows her head and sobs, her sorrow reflected in shots of scowling faces on a painting hung on the wall. Nola later seeks comfort from Clorinda who plays the double bass for her.

The aforementioned scene where Jamie forcibly takes Nola provides one of the most disturbing sequences in the film—one that even Lee did not fully understand when he wrote it.[19] The issues it raises include whether Nola has selfishly manipulated Jamie in begging him to come to her, whether she wanted to be taken, and whether Jamie has in fact raped her in disgust; these questions continue to reverberate well after the film has ended.

In an uncharacteristically perceptive soliloquy from the solitude of his garden, Greer concludes in mock-earnest fashion: "We let her create a . . . three-penis monster, and it was all our fault."

The next day Nola ritualistically scrapes the candles and melted wax from the headboard of her bed. She arranges a meeting with Greer under the Brooklyn Bridge, where she bids him adieu for good. Greer responds predictably with a childish tantrum. Along the waterfront, with the Manhattan skyline behind, Nola breaks similar news to Mars, whose last words are also humorously in character: "Please, baby, please, baby, please, baby, baby, please!" At the park bench, she tells Jamie that she will now see him exclusively, but in the meantime, she wants to remain celibate, confounding him again. In an unusual twist, Nola walks away in slow motion, only to return when Jamie calls out to her.

This apparently premature happy ending is given a final twist as we meet face-to-face in the loft once again with Nola, who sums up her situation:

> That celibacy thing didn't last too long. Who was I foolin'? As for Jamie, I just got a little crazy—should've never gone back in the first place. It was a momentary weakness. He wanted a wife, that mythic old-fashioned girl-next-door, but it's more than that. It's about control; my body, my mind. Who's gonna control it—them, or me? I am not a one-man woman. So there you have it from number of people who all claim to know what makes Nola Darling tick. I think they might know parts of me.

Having spoken, Nola rises and gets into bed, pulling the covers over her head as the camera takes in the headboard, glowing once more with numerous candles.

In *She's Gotta Have It,* director of photography Ernest Dickerson created some of the most exquisite black-and-white images of any film to emerge during the 1980s, including Francis Coppola's *Rumble Fish* and Martin Scorsese's *Raging Bull.* His lyrical lighting and intuitive use of warm-tone filters opens up the sensuous flesh tones of his subjects, particularly in the love scenes. The mixture of window light and artificial lighting lends the interior scenes a soft, yet crisp, natural glow. The mise-en-scène of certain three-shots recalls Welles's *Citizen Kane,* as when Nola and Jamie argue in the foreground over a third character, the lesbian Opal Gilstrap, appearing between them far in the background.

Each of the three male characters, if stereotypical, are nonetheless uniformly well drawn: the sensitive but dull Jamie; the amusing but ridiculous Mars;[20] and the physically attractive yet vapid Greer. Each lover can only partly satisfy Nola, therefore her need to continue relations with all three men makes sense because it is the sum of the three that makes a whole man. And it is easy to see why the three men "gotta have" Nola. Tracy Johns's earthy and self-assured rendition of Nola Darling is especially refreshing, a marked contrast to the archetypal fine-featured, straight-coiffured black mannequins of Hollywood mainstream films. Johns easily makes this "freak" a believable and sympathetic protagonist.

For all Lee's rhetoric about a New Black Cinema, his films betray a frankly old-fashioned movie sensibility. By the filmmaker's own accounts, the film takes many pages from the workbooks of the master film directors. In a technique borrowed from Martin Scorsese's *Raging Bull,* the opening shot of Nola Darling shifts imperceptibly from the standard 24 fps frame rate to slow motion. The stolen shots depicting Jamie and Nola's first Fulton Street meeting is derived from Godard's *Breathless* (1960). Lee himself has likened *She's Gotta Have It* to Kurosawa's *Roshomon*: "Every witness has his or her version, his or her own view of Nola Darling. A lot of views are contradictory but Nola herself is a contradiction."[21] Despite Lee's lofty assertions about his innovations, his films are often formulaic entertainments, similar in form and tone to the colorful but lightweight musicals he enjoyed in his youth. He described his film style as

a smorgasbord of different genres. If we saw something we liked then we would just use it. Like in *Rear Window* the first time you meet Grace Kelly is through a fog like in a dream. Jimmy Stewart's in his wheelchair and you see sweat dripping down his forehead then he opens his eyes and it goes to step printing. He opens his eyes and sees Grace—kiss. That's where we got the inspiration for the shots when I come down out the top of the frame and kiss Nola's breast.[22]

Lee succeeds admirably in creating an all-black universe without seeming contrived or forced. There are some scattered references to racially oriented current events of the day (for example, the Bumpors case) and some shots of racially motivated grafitti, but these are few and muted in tone. Lee nonetheless trumpets his opinions about the relative superiority of basketball club New York Knickerbockers through Mars's disparaging diatribe on white Boston Celtics star Larry Bird. Thus, the most insulting accusation Mars can hurl at Greer is "What do you know, you're a Celtics fan." In general, however, the strident racial polemics that characterize later films such as *School Daze* and *Do the Right Thing* do not muddy the laidback calm of this first feature.

She's Gotta Have It is in many ways Spike Lee's most satisfying film. *She's Gotta Have It* creates its own hermetic universe, with its timeless piano and horn jazz score reverberating in the distance, the langorous sex scenes in Nola's loft, and the noteworthy exclusion of all but black characters. The confessional quality of the film at first distances, then draws in the viewer to empathize face-to-face with the various characters as they express their plights. In some cases, the device of breaking the fourth wall becomes self-conscious, as in the succession of "dog" shots, but the actors' confidences with the audience provide an intimate look into the nature of contemporary sexual relationships.

Lee's next film, *School Daze*, was a chronicling of his college days at Morehouse. The film deals with prejudice within the black student body, pitting light-skinned "white wannabes" against dark-complected "jigaboos." The film was Lee's awkward first attempt at a feature-length musical format, a genre whose mastery proved elusive for the young director.

Lee proved himself a formidable talent with the release of his next picture, the controversial and forceful *Do the Right Thing*. His next film, *Mo' Better Blues*, was the story of a jazz horn player who suffers a career-ending lip injury at the hands of ruffians. *Jungle Fever*, Lee's subsequent attempt to mix themes of racism, drug abuse, and interracial adultery was only moderately successful. The $40 million epic *Malcolm X* represented the realization of a career-long dream for Lee, drew criticism from some Malcolm X contemporaries such as LeRoi Jones for its lack of authenticity, and was the first Lee feature to lose money at the box office. His following effort, *Crooklyn*, represented a conscious effort to return to a small-film format and a subject close to Lee's heart—the trials and tribulations of a 1970s family much like his own.

Lee has refused to join the Hollywood elite, which may be understandable in light of his jibes at movie luminaries like Spielberg. Lee frequently criticizes the American film industry for its censorship of black films, of being "afraid of having a film that would have majority black audiences." There can be no question, however, that Lee is now a fixture of the motion picture industry, and as such can no longer be considered an "independent" filmmaker.

Lee admits that he writes his films for black people, but he declines to assume a role as spokesperson. "But when we talk about a black film, you're carrying the whole burden of the black race on your shoulders. That's really unfair, though I can see their point because there are so few black films. So when one comes along, you put so much hope into it. It's the aspirations of a race upon you."[23]

NOTES

1. Lee has often decried the way white directors have interpreted stories of African-American origin, most notably Spielberg's treatment of *The Color Purple* and Alan Parker's *Mississippi Burning*.

2. Spike Lee, *Spike Lee's Gotta Have It* (New York: Simon and Schuster, 1987), p. 269.

3. Ibid., p. 26.

4. Ibid., p. 30.

5. Ibid., pp. 33–34.

6. While working in the equipment room, Lee became acquainted with Sara Driver, Jim Jarmusch's then-girlfriend and producer of his breakthrough independent feature, *Stranger Than Paradise*.

7. Spike Lee, interview. Larry Rohter, *New York Times*, August 10, 1986.

8. Spike Lee, interview. *Rolling Stone*, July 13, 1989, p. 107.

9. Spike Lee, interview. Simon Banner, *London Sunday Times*, March 8, 1987.

10. A format using single-perforated 16mm film with the normal 1:1.33 image area expanded to an aspect ratio of 1:1.66. Super 16 is often used by budget-conscious filmmakers to save money in production by using 16mm rather than the more expensive 35mm stock. The film is later blown up from 16mm to 35mm for exhibition prints. Super-16 is preferable for such enlargements as it does not necessitate cropping the top and bottom of the film frame.

11. Many of these black stereotypes would be lambasted by Robert Townshend in his own low-budget feature *Hollywood Shuffle*.

12. In some overseas markets, the title was changed to *Lola Darling* (*She's Gotta Have It*).

13. Lee, *Spike Lee's Gotta Have It*, p. 49.

14. Ibid., p. 49.

15. The take used for the film was one where Lee missed his mark and actually collided with the camera.

16. This scene initially brought the film an "X" rating from the MPAA. Lee finally managed to have the rating changed to the less restrictive "R" designation after agreeing to cut the scene by 50 percent.

17. This self-indulgent and clumsy homage to *The Wizard of Oz* is the weakest part of the film. The jarring Kodachrome-hues detract from the handsome monochromes of the rest of the film, and the poorly choreographed dance sequence completely stops the narrative as it flits about in an ill-conceived attempt to lighten spirits with an old-fashioned musical interlude. The presence of several tight shots of a Nagra tape recorder betrays a link to countless student films with similar juxtapositions of color and monochrome footage that shout at the viewer, "Look at us, we're making movies!" The sequence aptly demonstrates Lee's penchant for sentimental homages to motion pictures fondly remembered from his youth, a predilection that continues to figure in all of his feature film work.

18. Spike Lee, commentary. *She's Gotta Have It*, Criterion Collection laser disc, 1994.

19. Although Lee originally wrote this scene with Nola enjoying the violent sex and acknowledged in his journal that "IT'S IMPORTANT THAT THE CHARACTER OF NOLA DARLING NOT BE EXPLOITED" (caps his), Lee later admitted that the act depicted constituted a rape. Lee, *Spike Lee's Gotta Have It*, p. 87; Criterion Collection.

20. The Mars character enjoyed a life beyond *She's Gotta Have It* as a spokesman for the Nike Air Jordon shoe, as Spike Lee revealed a business acumen second only to George Lucas (who shrewdly marketed representations of all his most important *Star Wars* characters). Lee also opened up his own New York gift shop called Spike's Joint, in reference to the term he uses to label all of his motion pictures.

21. Lee, *Spike Lee's Gotta Have It*, p. 49.

22. Ibid., p. 56.

23. Ibid., p. 55.

CHAPTER 8

Lust's Labors Lost:
Working Girls
(1986)

USA: Unrated
Directed by Lizzie Borden
Cast in alphabetical order:
    Amanda Goodwin. . . . . Shawn
    Ellen McElduff. . . . . Susan
    Helen Nicholas. . . . . Mary
    Janne Peters. . . . . April
    Charles "Buddy" Rogers. . . . . unknown
    Louise Smith. . . . . Molly
Cinematography by Judy Irola
Music by David Van Tieghem
Written by
    Lizzie Borden
    Sandra Kay
Production designed by Kurt Ossenfort
Edited by Lizzie Borden
Produced by Lizzie Borden

> I get a lot of criticism for how I depict women because I don't portray idealized women's bodies or a male view of female sexuality. I like to see real women on-screen.
>
> Lizzie Borden[1]

Spike Lee's feature debut *She's Gotta Have It* was not the only New York–produced independent film to probe the often droll topic of sex in 1986. Across the East River in Manhattan, a decidedly less "sexy" vision of contemporary sexual mores was taking shape, this time from a distinctly feminine point of view. Filmmaker Lizzy Borden had unveiled her examination of middle-class prostitution in the form of a day in the life of a photographer who just happens to make ends meet practicing the oldest profession. Thus was born one of the year's most original and uncompromising films, *Working Girls*.

She was born *Linda* Borden in 1954, in the Detroit suburb of Birmingham, Michigan. Bored with her rather mundane given name, the rebellious Borden adopted the historic moniker Lizzie, "for the ax murderer, which of course I loved, but my parents hated."[2]

Borden studied painting and art history at Wellesley College in Massachussetts. After graduating Phi Beta Kappa, Borden enrolled at Queens College in New York to take advantage of the free studio space the school offered students. Though still unsure about a career as an artist, she began writing criticism for a respected art magazine when she was twenty-one.

Before this time, Borden had not been interested in film: "I wasn't one of those kids who grew up with Super-8, making my own little Spielberg-like epics at age seventeen. . . . But I saw a retrospective of Godard films at the Carnegie Hall cinema, and they just *grabbed* me. He threw away all the rules." Newly smitten with cinema, Borden taught herself filmmaking on her first project, *Regrouping*, a film "about being on the outside of a women's consciousness-raising group and feeling like an outsider."[3] The $10,000 film was crude by Borden's own estimation, but found screenings at the Edinburgh Film Festival and the Whitney Museum.

Borden's second film, *Born in Flames*, focused on a society in the wake of "a social-democratic cultural revolution. It was about women in the vanguard of trying to make the culture go back toward the left, and it showed how black women had no dialogue with white middle-class feminists."[4] The film featured female nonactors who spoke mostly unscripted dialogue that drew upon the women's real-life experiences. The film took four years to complete, and meanwhile Borden supported herself editing film for sculptor Richard Serra and for Alexandre Rockwell, an independent filmmaker. *Born in Flames* became something of a classic among feminist groups, winning first prize at the Women's Film Festival in Sceaux, France, and the jury prize for out-of-competition films at the Berlin Film Festival. Panned by many mainstream critics, *Born in Flames* was nonetheless embraced by many feminists as "one of the most dynamic feminist films ever made"[5] and "one of the most important films to come out in the '80s."[6]

Before making *Born in Flames*, Borden had met Margot St. James, the leader of the activist prostitutes' rights group Coyote (an acronym for "call off your old tired ethics"). She had planned a role for a prostitute in the film to be played by St. James herself, but the footage was excised from the final cut. In addition, Borden was surprised to discover that some of her own acquaintances "worked"—not in the streets but in small brothels. As she began to learn more about the illicit trade, she became intrigued. "Many women I met didn't at all fit the image of what I thought prostitutes would be," she reflected. "Many of them were making an economic choice based on other work options in this culture, and for many of them, renting their bodies was preferable to a 40-hour-a-week job."[7] The idea of prostitution as a viable temporary job alternative became a central theme for Borden's next film.

Borden began researching the sex trade by visiting a brothel when the madam was away and she became acquainted with the women and several of the clients. Borden knew that there was a film in her research, but she didn't want to make a documentary. Such an approach seemed too intrusive and would ultimately be limited to those acts that could be depicted outside the bedroom. Borden was fascinated with the workday routine of the prostitutes particularly, the obsessive emphasis on hygiene—the continual changing of towels, sheets, and condoms. Borden was also surprised to observe the relative power enjoyed by the women over their clients in the context of a brothel setting.

Borden taped conversations in the brothel and started writing scripts based on the dialogue. Since she sought greater control in the making of *Working Girls* than she could afford with her earlier films, she decided to build a set in her New York loft.

The alarm of a ticking clock awakens Molly, who rises from a bed she shares with her female lover. Molly, a young, middle-class white woman, rouses her partner's young daughter from her sleep, and begins her usual morning routine: washing up, fixing a light breakfast, sorting through slides and photographs, exchanging fond glances across the table with her lover. Molly packs a change of clothes in her bag and departs on her bicycle, wending her way through the New York streets.

She arrives at a nondescript building and enters what appears to be a comfortable waiting room. A phone rings repeatedly as Molly changes her clothes. The bathroom mirror reflects Molly lying on the floor struggling to insert a diaphragm as Gina, a tall brunette, pokes her head in to remind her of her imminent appointment with a Bob Burler. We begin to glean from the proceedings that this is no ordinary business.

At 10:20 A.M. Gina answers a knock at the door, admitting Dawn, a brassy young blonde who curses and complains loudly about the absent madam of the establishment: "She doesn't even tell her shrink that she's running a fucking whorehouse." Molly surmises that if the therapist knew, he might raise her rates. Dawn is upset because her boyfriend insisted on driving her to work, forcing her to duck into a catering shop where she pretends to work. Asked what he would do if he discovered Dawn's real profession, she answers flatly, "He'd fucking kill me."

The front door buzzer interrupts their chat, signaling Molly's first appointment of the day. She opens the door to greet Bob Burler, a bald man in a gray suit. Gina also greets him enthusiastically, but tellingly, Dawn avoids him. Molly brings a club soda, and he follows her upstairs to a bedroom, telling her some good business news as they make up the bed. She goes to the linen closet for a towel while he undresses.

Both standing naked, Bob and Molly strike a number of humorous poses before the bedroom mirror. An extreme closeup details the opening and unrolling of a condom. Bob grunts and writhes on top of Molly, murmuring her name as she impatiently checks the time on her wristwatch. Another closeup follows of Molly wrapping the used condom in a Kleenex. Molly goes back for a second towel, and brushes her teeth in the bathroom.

Downstairs, Dawn continues her complaints; Gina explains rates and girls over the phone to a prospective client. After Bob leaves, Molly asks the others to go along with her skimming, entering a half-hour session in the books instead of the full hour that Bob has paid for. Dawn tries to persuade Yale-graduate Molly to write a term paper for her. Molly and Dawn engage in a little shop talk; Dawn can't see why Molly continues to "see" Bob Burler, whom Molly confesses she finds "sweet." Dawn, on the other hand, finds his "sloppy kisses" disgusting. A close-up shows the pages of Molly's small accounting book. She enters $110 for Bob's session, plus a $20 tip.

A second customer, "Fagbag" Jerry arrives, embarrassing the women with crude hooker jokes. He doesn't appreciate Molly's correcting his English usage (he coins terms such as *aphrodisiAcal*), but requests her presence in a threesome with Gina. "I was sending him all my best hate signals," Molly sighs ruefully, but complies anyway, putting the phones on hold. Gina tries to persuade Jerry to take a "show" of feigned lovemaking between the women instead. Jerry declines, and Gina instead fellates him. He boasts of taking them to Italy, where "Rome is a whore." "That's Paris, Jerry. Henry Miller," replies Molly. Jerry ignores her, and asks Gina to perform "around the world," which she snickeringly fakes for an additional $30. He roughly pulls Gina around to enter her without a "rubber," which she is quick to remind him "will cost $30 extra." Afterward, we see Gina washing out her diaphragm while Molly tries to treat the "hickey" Jerry has given her.

A more detailed picture of the brothel emerges, with Molly clearly a newcomer who is learning the ropes from veteran Gina and hard-edged Dawn. Hanging around the waiting room, Molly wants Gina to reassure her that the madam will not discover their skimming, and tries rubbing a silver spoon on her neck to make her hickey disappear. They talk about one of the older "girls," who is turning forty-five. Gina answers a call from a john who wants to know if any of the women will do "Greek," a request that draws a resounding no. Gina calls out an order for lunch, while Dawn fields a call from madam Lucy's boyfriend, Miles. Gina discusses Miles, who met Lucy as a trick when the madam herself worked as a prostitute.

In a series of extreme closeups, the women munch sandwiches, and weigh the pros and cons of being a "working girl," discussing other career options. Dawn declares her aspiration to be a lawyer, which draws laughter from the others. The women scramble to clean up lunch as the buzzer brings an end to their conversation.

"It's John," announces Gina as she opens the door. John sits with the women sipping a drink, talking nervously. When Gina presses him about whom he would "like to see," he excuses himself to "put money in the parking meter." Gina and Dawn affirm that his last-minute bailouts are a common ritual. Gina describes Molly's physical attributes over the phone to "Fantasy Fred," who promises to arrive shortly. A man named Jay arrives, holding a briefcase that he refuses to let go. After eyeing the three women, he chooses to go upstairs with Dawn. Gina reveals to Molly how she lost her boyfriend after telling him about her "work." Molly admits that she hasn't told her lover Diane.

Dawn reappears and informs Gina that John has changed his mind and is asking for her instead, declaring that there are some things she just won't do. Gina will do this one "off the books." Picking up the end of Gina and Molly's conversation, Dawn adds paradoxically, "I believe in fidelity. In the five years I've gone out with Jeff, I haven't cheated on him once."

Fantasy Fred arrives (offscreen, Dawn shouts "yabadabadoo") and follows Molly up to the bedroom. While getting the requisite towel, Molly peeps in on Gina and Jake. She is spanking him with a Ping-Pong paddle as he babbles lurid schoolgirl tales. Returning to Fred, Molly asks him to "make himself completely comfortable" (the "girls'" euphemism for undressing), but he refuses. Instead, Fred wants her to play doctor with him, pretending to be a blind virgin whose eyesight is restored after having intercourse for the first time. Doctor Fred promises to show her "something very hard, but it will give you a lot of pleasure." "But Doctor," Molly asks, unimpressed, "why isn't it hard?" Fred then asks for fellatio, but looks distressed when Molly reaches for the condom. He lurches on top of her, and, on cue, Molly's sight miraculously returns. Fred asks if he can see Molly again.

Back downstairs, Gina smokes a marijuana cigarette with another "girl," offering a toke to Molly. The women joke about the naïveté of madam Lucy, who just flounces through the door at that moment. She fusses and fumes, reprimanding the women for their smoking and sloppiness. An unctuous social climber, Lucy can't wait to show off the clothes she has bought (with the profits from her business—a fact not lost on her employees). She answers the phone in her characteristically saccharine greeting, "What's new and different?"

In the kitchen, Gina and Molly stick candles in a birthday cake Lucy has bought for one of the nightshift "girls." Lucy pompously lectures the women about the importance of maintaining a veneer of "class." A dapper client, Robert, arrives, followed by the older businessman Joseph (played by the noted documentarist Richard Leacock); they join Lucy and the others in the waiting area. Lucy instructs Molly to take Joseph to the "jungle room," and tells her where she can find rope with which to tie him up. Meanwhile Gina takes Robert upstairs. Looking over the books, Lucy scolds Dawn for her low take. Molly comes to her defense, and is in turn admonished for forgetting to bring her garter belt and stockings.

Some rollicking music sets the tone for our purviewing of Joseph's "light dominant" session while he shouts mock protests. Afterward, Joseph asks to see her "on the outside" and Molly adds the trick to the tally in her book.

Downstairs, Lucy shouts at Dawn for cursing at her client; the insulted fat man descends the stairs, shoves Dawn, and threatens to report the whole operation to the police. Lucy eventually mollifies him.

A well-dressed black woman arrives and follows Lucy upstairs for an interview. Gina greets Lucy's young suitor Miles while Molly fixes him a drink. Dawn leaves for her college class. The black woman, Debbie, meets with Lucy's approval and stays for a shift at Lucy's behest. The other women supply Debbie with condoms and tips for dealing with the demanding madam.

An upscale black businessman arrives and sits with the others. Debbie averts her eyes, feelings apparently hurt, when Charles passes her over and asks who else is available; he ends up leaving. Lucy attempts to console her by explaining that it's nothing personal—black women just aren't as in demand. Lucy asks if Molly will stay an extra hour to see a special client named Neal.

Molly takes orders for a contraceptive run to the local drugstore. On her way back to work, Molly stops for a moment's reflection in a park, wistfully watching the children and their mothers.

Back at the brothel, the aforementioned April has arrived. It is her birthday that others prepare to celebrate—her forty-fifth. A prostitute named Marilyn calls in sick, prompting Lucy to plead with Molly to work a second shift. Molly is worn out and agrees to work only a few hours extra. New "girl" Mary has shown up for work. Lucy gives her instructions on how to dress—"as if you just come from lunch with your mother and are on your way to meet your boyfriend."

Upstairs, Molly lounges in bed with bearded professor Neal. He gives her a shirt of his that she had liked. Molly, in turn, gives him pointers on how to make a pass at a date. "Is she going to expect me to sleep with her?" he asks nervously.

The next client, Bongo, who customarily romps with numerous "girls" at a time, arrives and goes upstairs. Molly tells Mary a little about the business before they go up to give Bongo a "show" (feigned lesbian love-making). April indiscreetly sets up a drug deal over the phone. After their session, Mary is shaken, asking Molly, "Do you think he knew I didn't like it?" Molly assures her, "He doesn't want to know."

Molly telephones her roommate and leaves a message, telling her that she will be working late. Some Asian businessmen arrive, and the women line up to let them make their selections. One chooses Mary, the other goes with Molly. He gives her trouble, first refusing a shower, then demanding she fellate him. When he refuses to wear a condom, she perfunctorily satisfies him manually.

Hurrying downstairs, Molly finds that April has placed the phones on hold—one of Lucy's pet peeves. Lucy bursts in in a huff, angry at the unrepentant April because she has not been able to get through on the telephone. She chides Miles about giving his wife more gifts than her. The women present April with the cake, singing "Happy Birthday." April gives Lucy advice on how to get Miles to leave his wife and marry her.

Next appears Paul, an attractive composer musician, and Molly undresses while he suggests "getting together on the outside." Molly tells him that would be unlikely, considering his attitudes toward women. "I don't think you see us as equals," she explains. "As long as I'm paying for this, we're not equals," he replies. Paul's charm quickly turns to rough unpleasantness, and Molly pushes him off and gazes away.

In the bathroom, Molly splashes water on her face and bursts into tears. It is now late in the evening, and she pleads with Lucy to let her leave. Unfortunately, Lucy has already booked her into another appointment. In the waiting room, Mary gets an urgent call from her child, who is at home alone and frightened. Mary becomes upset, then quiet and sullen. Charles pops back in, but doesn't see anything to his liking and quickly departs. Lucy scolds Mary for taking the call. "Yeah, Mary, don't you know," Molly spits back sarcastically, "working girls aren't supposed to have children—or periods—or bad moods."

Lucy is surprised to see a bald older businessman at the door: "Oh, hi, Elliot," she laughs nervously, "how did you get by the doorman?" He exchanges awkward salutations with April, suggesting his previous visits have not always been successful. In bed with Molly, Elliot asks the question of the hour, "Could we meet outside of here? I know lots of guys must ask you that." After their session, he slips her his business card.

Molly relaxes in a bath, tired and worn out. She totals her sessions in the black book ($880) and counts her day's earnings—well over $,1000. After stuffing most of it into her wallet, she tucks Elliot's card in as well. Wheeling her bike out to the waiting room, Molly hands Lucy her part of the day's take, and learns that Mary has left for good. In the film's final exchange, Molly voices a theme that has developed throughout the picture—that it is not the men, but the madam who exploits the "working girls":

> **LUCY:** Gee, Molly, you did very well today. See it wasn't so bad? You made a lot of money.
>
> **MOLLY:** I made a lot of money for you. Lucy, have you ever heard of surplus value?[8]
>
> **LUCY:** Don't be patronizing. I went to a good school too.
>
> **MOLLY:** I'm leaving.
>
> **LUCY:** OK, babe. See you next week.
>
> **MOLLY:** No you won't. I'm not coming back, Lucy.
>
> **LUCY:** Mollie—honey, you're just tired. You go home and take a nice warm bath. You're going to feel just fine in the morning. Molly? Molly, you can't just leave—what about your regulars? Molly, you can't walk out on me, you know I'm short on girls.

Molly walks her bicycle out, wheels clicking; the door slams behind her. It's nearly 11:00 P.M. Riding through the inky night, she breathes in the cool night air, free of the confines of the brothel. She stops to deposit her money at a bank teller machine, picks up a bouquet at an all-night market, and nestles into bed behind her lover. The film ends with a freeze frame of her face in close-up, eyes wide open, then closing as the credits roll out.

Working Girls challenges one of the oldest myths of the movies: that of the glamorous prostitute with the heart of gold, who toils in the oldest profession until rescued by her Prince Charming. It is an absurdly simple-minded fairy tale used with dismaying success in one of the highest grossing films of the nineties, *Pretty Woman* (which brought Julia Roberts to stardom). On the contrary, many sociologists and reformers see prostitution as an ugly and debilitating social evil to be eradicated. But it is not Lizzie Borden's intent to pull back the curtain and expose prostitution as the abusive, dehumanizing trade many believe it to be. Rather, Borden presents prostitution as merely a "living," an alternative type of temporary employment akin to other types of paid servitude: waitressing, clerical work, and professional child care. By the film's end, Mollie is clearly leaving the sweatshop environment of the brothel for good, although it appears that by keeping one of her client's business cards, she intends to continue "working," this time for herself, on a freelance basis. Thus, *Working Girls* is not about the degrading nature of commercial sex but, rather, the drudgery of mind-dulling work.

One remarkable feature of *Working Girls* is the fashion in which it de-eroticizes sex. There is nudity and plenty of sexual activity, none of which can be described as arousing. The brothel environment hardly embodies the stereotypical New Orleans image of red velvet curtains, Victorian furniture, and sweeping staircases; instead it resembles any small office. The lighting is flat and unflattering overall, not unlike the ambient fluorescent illumination in an industrial setting. The key activities are not the ménage à trois or the orgy, but rather the routine of any forty-hour-week business: supply errands, fast food runs, birthday parties, and working shifts. The tedium quickly becomes obvious as we see everyday rituals played out repeatedly, from the greetings, drinks, and coded cues ("make yourself completely comfortable") to the continual changing towels and condoms.

There is no eye candy in this film: the visual aspects of the film and its sex scenes are consciously rendered in an unaesthetic, harsh light, while the color scheme of the brothel is uniformly drab, in variations of olive green, puce, or gray. One of the interesting aspects of *Working Girls* is its subversion of the act of male "scopophilia," or pleasure in looking—in this case, at the act of sex. Depictions of sex in the film do not function according to one accepted notion of the "male gaze," as described in a much-discussed 1975 essay by Laura Mulvey, in that "the spectator identifies with the main male protagonist, he projects his look on that of his like, his screen surrogate, so that the power of the male protagonist as he controls events coincides with the active power of the erotic look, both giving a satisfying sense of omnipotence."[9] Rather, the male viewer who identifies with the clients in *Working Girls*, in witnessing the events that transpire in the brothel, himself experiences feelings of his own impotence, both physically and socially. The men often seek approval and authority from the women, as when professor Neal gives Molly his own shirt and asks for dating advice. Others often appear to look foolish and easily duped. For example, when Jerry requests analingus from Gina, she pretends to comply and charges him $30 extra, but in fact deceives him by using a finger rather than her tongue to administer the act. When an oafish Japanese client refuses to wear a condom, Molly simply denies him sexual intercourse and masturbates him instead. And when Fantasy Fred boasts of his sexual prowess in the midst of an elaborate make-believe session, Molly breaks the fantasy to blithely ask why his penis has not become erect.

Unlike the criticism that Susan Seidelman's film *Smithereens* drew for what some saw as the excessive moralizing of its narrative, *Working Girls* was condemned for its refusal to judge its characters and their chosen avocation. Borden acknowledged having taken heat from women's activist groups for her refusal to moralize, from many of the same feminists who championed Borden's previous film, *Born in Flames*:

> I've been attacked by everyone; by feminists who say, "You're soft-peddling prostitution; prostitution is *wrong*," and by spiritual women who say you can't have all these sexual encounters without doing damage to your soul. . . . What strikes me is that people who would morally judge sex without feeling during prostitution don't judge the same act in other circumstances: for example, a woman decides to give her husband a quick fuck because otherwise he's going to be pushing up against her all night, not letting her sleep; she's not into it, but it's quicker and easier to get him off, to get it over with, than to be continually dealing with it. How many times does that happen in this culture?[10]

To her credit, Borden points a finger not at the sexism of men but at the dehumanizing management-labor structure of the capitalist system. Subverting the conventional stereotype, her prostitutes do not harbor any animosity toward the opposite sex. Rather, it is management—in the form of madam Lucy—whom they conspire against. "The real fight, as in any employment situation," Borden acknowledges, "is with the employer—in prostitution, the pimp or madam."[11] Hence, with *Working Girls*, Borden seems to be saying that prostitution is simply another industry wherein employees toil as drones, a career option as unsatisfying as other typically mindless jobs such as assembly-line work and waitressing. Indeed, notes Borden, "nobody criticizes the forty-hour workweek. Nobody criticizes the fact that for the most part people are trained into positive thinking about jobs that don't make use of half their talents."[12]

Working Girls trades on the old cliché that men see prostitutes for companionship rather than sex. Many of the clients share a common desire to see Molly "outside" the brothel, as a girlfriend. This may be because the "working girls" of the film are depicted as women rather than as addicts or sluts; they all appear to share a middle-class background. Only one of them appears to use drugs, and most of them carry on "normal" lives and relationships outside of the brothel. There is a veneer of social class at work here. Though obviously a kept mistress, the madam pretends to be a society woman at home in Bloomingdales and Gucci.

Despite the film's dynamic subversion of erotic elements in its examination of the oldest profession, *Working Girls* was closely scrutinized and judged to be pornographic by the Screen Actors Guild. This was an unexpected benefit, as it exempted the film from SAG's required pay scales.

(Borden paid the actors SAG wages nonetheless.) Before it could debut at the Toronto Film Festival, *Working Girls* was called up for review by the Ontario Censor Board and refused exhibition until Borden physically placed tape over the offending "handjob" footage (to spare the costly print the irreparable damage of physical cutting). Borden encountered further problems when she tried to seek an "R" rating for the film from the Motion Picture Association of America. In order to avoid the much-maligned "X" rating, she "found out that so much would need to be cut . . . that there'd hardly be a film left."[13] Ultimately, as with *She's Gotta Have It*, the film's distributor demanded that *Working Girls* be reedited to tone down some of its more explicit scenes.

The success of *Working Girls* brought offers from Hollywood, but it was four years until the release of Borden's next feature, *Love Crimes*, this time funded and produced under the auspices of Miramax Pictures. The story centers on a tough female district attorney (played by Sean Young) who investigates a man who poses as a famous photographer in order to victimize women sexually and financially. When the women—each somehow sexually fulfilled by the encounters—prove reluctant to press charges, the DA arranges to meet the man. Of course, she finds herself confronting the same submissive desires.

The film was not successful, perhaps because *Love Crimes*, unlike Borden's previous films, seems to want it both ways—as a feminist look at intergender politics, and as a Hollywood-style sex thriller in the mold of *Basic Instinct* or *Body of Evidence*. Borden, however, blamed the failure on creative concessions she was forced to make in casting and postproduction: "I cringe sometimes when when I look at *Love Crimes* because I know what I wanted that film to be."[14]

Borden has since worked on a variety of projects, ranging from a documentary on phone sex for the Playboy Channel to a short dramatic film entitled *Let's Talk About Sex* that ran as one part of a triptich entitled *Erotique*.[15]

In light of her recent difficulties in floating a feature-length Hollywood-financed project, Borden has considered a return to no-budget independent filmmaking as a way to continue her unique directorial approach. The irony is not lost on Borden. As an artist who spent much of her early motion picture career as a film editor, she noted with some resignation: "The reality is, when I came to Hollywood, I stopped having final cut."[16]

NOTES

1. Victoria A. Brownworth, "Working Girl," *The Advocate*, August 23, 1994, p. 83.

2. Lizzie Borden, "Grass-roots Filmmaking." In John Russo, ed., *Making Movies* (New York: Fireside, 1989), p. 70.

3. Ibid., p. 70.

4. Lizzise Borden, interview with Richard K. Ferncase, 1990.

5. Brownworth, "Working Girl," p. 89.

6. Ibid., p. 89.

7. Lizzie Borden, interview. Coco Fusco, *Afterimage*, Fall 1987, p. 46.

8. In Marxian economics, the part of the value of a commodity that exceeds the cost of labor is regarded as the profit of the capitalist.

9. Laura Mulvey, "Visual Pleasure and Narrative Cinema." In Gerald Mast, ed., *Film Theory and Criticism*, 4th ed. (New York: Oxford University Press, 1992), p. 749.

10. Lizzie Borden, interview. Scott McDonald, *A Critical Cinema 2: Conversations with Independent Filmmakers* (Berkeley: University of California Press, 1992), p. 259.

11. Fusco, *Afterimage*, p. 47.

12. McDonald, *A Critical Cinema*, p. 259.

13. Ibid., p. 259.

14. Brownworth, "Working Girl," p. 84.

15. The other segments are by Monika Treut and Clara Law.

16. Brownworth, "Working Girl," p. 89.

CHAPTER 9

Oddities and Odysseys:
The Thin Blue Line
(1988)

USA: 1988

35mm Color

Directed by Errol Morris

Interviews with:

Randall Adams, David Harris, Gus Rose, Jackie Johnson, Marshall Touchton, Dale Holt, Sam Kittrell, Hootie Nelson, Dennis Johnson, Floyd Jackson, Edith James, Dennis White, Don Metcalfe, Emily Miller, R.L. Miller, Elba Carr, Micael Randell, and Melvyn Carson Bruder

Cinematography by

Robert Chappell

Stefan Czapsky

Music by Philip Glass

Production designed by Teddy Bafaloukos

> We had a six-minute rule: "shut up and let people talk for six minutes and they'll show you how crazy they really are."
>
> Errol Morris[1]

Errol Morris was stunned. Randall Dale Adams, falsely accused, convicted, and imprisoned nearly thirteen years for the killing of a Dallas police officer, was getting ready to return to the courtroom. Adams wasn't going back again to stand trial in that case. He was preparing to file suit against the man who made the film instrumental in freeing him—Errol Morris.

It's another twist in a bizarre series of events for Morris, one of the more offbeat documentary filmmakers to emerge in the eighties. More interested in finding the whereabouts of Einstein's embalmed brain or probing into the case of an Old English sheepdog charged with murder, Morris eschews the social problems, environmental concerns, and political topics of the traditional documentarist. More than mere records of people, places, and things, his films reflect his own idiosyncratic personality. "There's no reason why documentaries can't be as personal as fiction filmmaking and bear the imprint of those who made them," he explains. "Truth isn't guaranteed by style or expression. It isn't guaranteed by anything."[2]

The tradition of documentary filmmaking goes back to the Lumière brothers' first *actualités* of 1896. These early reproductions of unstaged events enthralled audiences; one Lumière film, *The Arrival of a Train*, sent viewers fleeing in panic from the approaching locomotive on the screen. The first real nonfiction film doctrines were set forth some thirty years later by Russian filmmaker Dziga Vertov, whose Kino-Pravda series of newsreels presaged the "film-truth" school of documentary filmmaking. Vertov went beyond merely recording his subjects, however, applying Sergei Eisenstein's theories of metaphoric montage to nonfiction filmmaking and employing self-reflexive photographic techniques to comment on scenes of everyday life. In his 1929 film *Man with the Movie Camera*, Vertov uses an eye motif to link otherwise unrelated shots of windows, doors, and like subjects superimposed with images of a camera and operator recording the scenes. Edited together in a new context, these images imparted poetic meaning to mundane objects. Vertov's license with montage was not, however, what the Scotsman John Grierson had in mind when he coined the actual term "documentary" in 1926. Grierson was referring to a work by Robert Flaherty, who made what is generally acknowledged to be the first important nonfiction film, *Nanook of the North* (1922). This seminal work, featuring lengthy takes of an Eskimo hunter and his family going about their daily activities, was the embodiment of what Grierson termed "the creative treatment of reality." Indeed, it was necessary for him to treat his subject with creativity. Bound by the limitations of slow film and cumbersome equipment, his subjects often rehearsed their roles for the camera.

The advent of lightweight cameras, portable crystal-sync tape recorders, and sensitive film stock in the late 1940s and 1950s was a boon to documentarists, freeing them to use more spontaneous means of recording their subjects. As a result, the accepted paradigm for documentary motion pictures has become the style known as cinema verité, or "camera truth."

This approach strives for immediacy and authenticity, eschewing the use of any preconceived narrative of concepts concerning the material. Cinema verité and direct-cinema adherents generally frown on the use of insert shots, third-person narration, manipulative editing, or setup interviews to manipulate or comment overtly on a subject. Thus, the hallmarks of a cinema verité film include a grainy, shaky picture, long sequence shots, and ambient sounds of subjects going about various activities.

By his own admission, Morris had little affinity for this approach, setting out deliberately to break the accepted formulae: "What I do has nothing to do with cinema-verité. The idea isn't to creep up on people or to use low or available light. We go in with a lot of equipment, the camera is on a tripod, and the person who speaks to the camera is perfectly aware of what is going on. In some sense, he is performing for the camera."[3]

Morris often found himself at odds with cinematographers who disagree with his interview methods. He fired four camera persons who attempted to zoom in on subjects. During a session with Adams, Morris encouraged the wronged man to open up by sympathizing verbally with him. This outraged the cameraman, to whom Morris replied, "if I wanted a moral philosopher, I would hire Immanuel Kant." Morris found a new operator to finish the interviews.[4]

Indeed, philosophy was more important than filmmaking technique to Morris, who preferred trilobites to movies as a boy growing up in suburban Long Island. He graduated with honors from the University of Wisconsin with a BA in history, and, following an unsuccessful stint at Princeton, he attended UC Berkeley where he entered a PhD program in philosophy. Though absorbed with philosophical issues, he found academic life to be a less-than-nurturing experience:

> Almost everything I do now in my work is about epistemic concerns: how do we come by certain types of knowledge? Take the insanity plea—we talk about insane acts and insane people. . . . I wrote an essay on the insanity plea and movie monsters and certain mechanistic fantasies we have about criminal behavior. I very much wanted to write a doctoral thesis on this stuff, and it hurt my feelings when Berkeley just sort of kicked my ass out of there.[5]

Turning his back on the "world of pedants," he began to frequent the Pacific Film Archive, an art cinema and library that frequently screened esoteric motion pictures. The archive's director, Tom Luddy, introduced Morris to the German filmmaker Werner Herzog, whose unusual obsessive themes meshed with Morris's own leanings.[6]

Morris's research on the insanity plea took him back to Wisconsin, where he conducted several interviews with Ed Gein, a notorious convicted mass murderer, grave robber, and amateur taxidermist who inspired both *Psycho*

(1960) and *The Texas Chainsaw Massacre* (1974). Morris discovered that the small town of Plainfield, Wisconsin, alone had a recent record of several multiple killers within a single decade. It was as if Gein had spawned a cult of murderers in that Wisconsin town. Herzog, fascinated with Morris's inquiries into American lunacy, planned to meet Morris in Plainfield in the summer of 1975. Then they would proceed to the town cemetery, brandishing shovels to solve a question that bothered them both—did Ed Gein actually exhume the body of his mother? Herzog waited in vain for his accomplice; Morris thought better of the enterprise and stayed home. He continued to research the subject and wanted to make a film on Gein entitled *Digging up the Past*.

One day Morris noticed a newspaper article that mentioned that a number of residents of a certain Southern town tried to collect insurance benefits after mysteriously suffering severed limbs. Morris learned that the town was Vernon, Florida (population 883), and traveled there to have a look around. After reading the courthouse records and questioning a few residents, Morris received at least one death threat; he headed back to Berkeley to write a feature screenplay on "Nub City—about people who in order to achieve the American dream literally become a fraction of themselves."[7]

Morris had made little progress on the script when he was struck with an entirely different idea: "I saw an article that appeared in *The San Francisco Chronicle* that was entitled 'Five Hundred Dead Pets To Napa,' and it was the story of a pet cemetery that had failed financially. The pets buried were to be exhumed and transported in refrigerator trucks north to Bubbling Well Pet Memorial Park, which was a successful pet cemetery."[8] This would be the germ for his first film, *Gates of Heaven*. In light of Morris's desultory interests, Werner Herzog was skeptical about the project. "You'll never make a film," he predicted, "but if you do I'll come and eat my shoe at the premiere." Morris would make the film; meanwhile, his other projects would have to wait.

In *Gates of Heaven*, Morris carefully composes and lights his scenes, using a controlled interview technique reminiscent of television's *60 Minutes*. Instead of a question-and-answer session, however, the subjects are allowed to reflect and ramble at length without prompting or prodding. The speakers are never identified by subtitles; rather, the viewer learns their names as they talk about one another.

Gates of Heaven opens with Floyd "Mac" McClure, professed animal lover and would-be proprietor of the pet cemetery of his dreams. He reminisces fondly about his burial of a favorite pet collie and grumbles righteously about the "glue factory" rendering industry. We meet his fellow investors who, though initially charmed into his idealistic venture, appear chagrined and bewildered before the camera. Slowly, it is revealed through the testimony of the various subjects that the cemetery is losing money. The never-seen landowner Dunton emerges as the villain in this dream gone sour when, according to McClure, "They decided I should open one grave site and put several pets into one grave and close it. To me that only spelled one thing—'let's get all the bucks we can out of this.' "

Mac's vision evaporates and the animals are exhumed and sent to the Bubbling Well park, run by Calvin and Scottie Harberts along with their sons, Phil and Danny. Unlike Floyd McClure, Cal Harberts is unflinchingly pragmatic about the business of burial: "We're often asked 'why is your business apparently successful where others have failed?' The only answer I can give is a very obvious one, and that is that we have tried to follow sound business practices, where it's quite obvious that other pet cemeteries that have now failed have not." Other family members are equally unsentimental. Phil, home with his parents after an unsuccessful stint in the insurance business, expounds W. Clement Stone's Positive Mental Attitude credo, while Danny stoically reflects on his lot as second-in-command at the cemetery. While Danny muses about the nature of dreams, Phil states numbly, "our mind is like a computer."

Morris's ironic juxtapositions give *Gates of Heaven* its distinct bittersweet flavor. The film is not above overt visual commentary, as when the handicapped McClure turns away for the first time in his wheelchair ruing, "I was not only broke but brokenhearted." Phil mouths empty platitudes ("success is like a journey") over images of a refrigerator truck lumbering along the road. Shots of marker plates enshrining "Tippins," "Miss Muffet," and other deceased pets provide a curious counterpoint to the elder Harberts's descriptions of his diligent efforts "to break up the rows of little headstones which can be monotonous and not very appealing." The most droll and touching moment comes when Danny stands alone upon the hill overlooking the cemetery and plays his electric guitar, sending blasts of amplified rock chords booming across the barren valley.

Gates of Heaven is ultimately not about pet cemeteries; rather, it is about loneliness and longing, of fragile dreams tempered by hard realities. The characters are isolated from one another, framed in static medium shots. They are "people who seem to be talking into a void," observes Morris. Mac moons over his failed pet cemetery and rails bitterly against the rendering plants. Danny Harberts muses over a lost love from his college days and abandoned aspirations for fame as a rock star, as he plucks notes from a wistful Jefferson Airplane song on his acoustic guitar. Phil expounds his hollow motivational doctrines behind a trophy-cluttered desk, but appears less than convinced himself. Middle-aged couples in polyester speak solemn eulogies for their dead pets. The film closes with a susurrus of insects hissing over the haunting images of neglected animal statuary, in a scene as silent and disquieting as a Georgio de Chirico painting.

True to his word, Werner Herzog feasted ceremoniously on a parboiled desert boot at the Berkeley premiere of *Gates of Heaven*, an event documented in the Les Blank film *Werner Herzog Eats His Shoe*. Its auspicious debut notwithstanding, the $125,000 *Gates of Heaven* was not widely screened despite its many favorable reviews. Herzog called the film "the only authentic State of the Union address," while no less a figure than Roger Ebert gave it his highest praise. But even as critics lauded the film, it languished, "sitting on a dusty shelf somewhere," says Morris, enjoying "no real distribution."[9]

In 1979, Morris returned to nose around the town of Vernon. Suspicious townspeople accused him of wanting to exploit "the Nub City stuff" and after a few months, Morris again left town. Undaunted, he came back a year later, this time with a film crew of NYU graduates and funding from public broadcasting affiliate WNET and a German television firm. Morris was sternly advised by the "king of the nubbies" to cease his inquiries and leave town within twenty-four hours. When Morris failed to comply, cinematographer Ned Burgess was nearly run down by a mysterious truck. A rattled Morris began filming a series of unrelated interviews with some of Vernon's body-intact inhabitants, in an effort to get something on film to satisfy his backers.

The resulting sixty-minute film *Vernon, Florida* ultimately featured no nubbies, evolving instead into a train of rambling accounts delivered by some of Vernon's other colorful residents. The film begins as a beatup truck ambles down deserted streets ominously spraying clouds of poison spray; a disembodied voice wonders aloud, "Reality? You mean this is the real world?" This may or not be reality; from the first scene, however, we know we are firmly in Morris territory.[10]

The men pictured in *Vernon, Florida* beam and cackle over their various obsessions. One stands before a local filling station posing the question: "Ever see a man's brains?" He moves his hands and feet in different directions to demonstrate independent parts of the human brain. Offering proof, he writes the word "bullshit" with one hand while the other scrawls "dogshit."

Another tells elaborate fish tales. One day as he reels in a catch, the hooked fish escapes into the carcass of a submerged mule. When the man hauls the mule up on the shore to land the fish, he is startled by a fluttering sound within the body. Inside he finds 114 perch.

A couple displays a jar of radioactive sand collected during a visit to White Sands Nuclear Testing Grounds. They make a remarkable claim: the sand is "growing." In a few years time, the three-fourths-full jar will be brimming with the magic silica.

One particularly obsessive gentleman, Henry Shipes, loves to hunt wild turkeys. "I can't tell you how I feel. It's just a hell of a sport," he enthuses, showing off his trophies of preserved turkey feet and wattles.

After the completion of *Vernon, Florida*, Morris tried to float a number of screenwriting deals without success. He sustained himself for a year and a half as a private detective investigating Wall Street trading and takeover cases, and claims to have endured intense stress during the expensive Italian luncheons he shared with investigatees and their lawyers. "The people I was trying to interview seemed to have a hearty appetite," he recalled. His most valuable piece of equipment turned out to be neither a gun nor a camera; rather, it was "the stain remover I carried in my brief-case."[11]

> Someday a car will stop to pick me up that I never thumbed.
> Yes—fate, or some mysterious force, can put the finger on you
> or me for no good reason at all.
>
> From the film *Detour* (Ulmer, 1946)

Errol Morris's time as a detective would prepare him for his next film, *The Thin Blue Line*, which some have called the first film noir documentary. Film noir, literally "black film," was originally a term coined by French moviegoers to describe the distinctly dark and cynical films that came out of Hollywood in the years following the Second World War. Film noir often employed the mystery genre, particularly the hard-boiled detective popularized by Dashiel Hammett and Raymond Chandler. Film noir pictures like *Double Indemnity* (1944), *The Big Sleep* (1945), and *Detour* (1946) usually portrayed neurotic and sordid characters inhabiting a shadowy urban world of crime and corruption. Uncontrollable events occurred in an ineluctable universe of doom, enveloping characters in a downward spiral of irreversible catastrophes. Morris would discover a character mired in a such a universe in Dallas County.

As with *Vernon, Florida*, *The Thin Blue Line* originated from a wholly disparate starting point. Funding from the Corporation for Public Broadcasting allowed Morris to journey to Texas and begin a project he called "Dr. Death," about a Dallas psychiatrist named James Grigson, who was frequently called upon to give routinely damning testimony in death-penalty court cases.

Texas law dictates that a death penalty may be only imposed when a jury is confident that a felon will commit further violence. As one of the "killer shrinks," Grigson was regularly commissioned to interview a convict and report his findings to the court. Grigson nearly always found the accused to be remorseless, and therefore likely to kill again. The jury would then be able by law to return a guilty verdict, effectively condemning the prisoner to the electric chair. Grigson cooperated wholeheartedly with Morris, and encouraged him to visit the convicts he helped put on death row. Not surprisingly, all of the twenty-five felons there protested their innocence. The testimony of one prisoner, Randall Dale Adams, raised some disturbing questions in Morris's mind.

Court records showed that in the spring of 1977, Adams had been convicted and sentenced to die for the murder of a Dallas police officer, Robert Wood, committed the year prior. Wood and his partner Teresa Turko had stopped a car that was driving with its headlights off. When Wood approached the driver, he was shot five times and left to die as the car streaked away. Adams told Morris that he was framed, and blamed the killing on "the kid" David Harris, who was the key witness for the prosecution. Morris went to Austin and read transcripts of the hearings and found inconsistencies. He arranged to talk with David Harris in a bar outside the town of Beaumont. It was then that Morris began to suspect that Adams was indeed the victim.

In October 1976, Randall Adams and his brother made a stopover in Dallas on the way to California. The stop seemed fortuitous, Adams recalls: "I'm not in town half a day and I've got a job. It's just—everything clicked. It's as if I was meant to be here." On November 27, 1976, Adams left work and ran out of gas. A young man, David Harris, offered him a ride, and Adams accepted.

As *The Thin Blue Line* begins, David Harris offers his own chilling account: "This all started the day I ran away from home. I took a pistol of my dad's and a shotgun, and took a neighbor's car, broke in their house or something and got the keys—I forget exactly what it was—and ended up going to Dallas." Together they spent the rest of the evening drinking beer and smoking marijuana at a drive-in movie. Afterward, Harris dropped Adams off at his motel room and drove away. Later that night, Robert Wood was shot to death.

The Thin Blue Line reconstructs events surrounding the murder according to various spoken accounts of several detectives and witnesses. Police officials are disturbed that Wood's killing goes unsolved for weeks. Harris is arrested in the town of Vidor, after boasting that he "offed a pig" in Dallas. Immune from capital punishment as a juvenile, Harris turns state's evidence and implicates Randall Adams in the killing. Eyewitnesses required to make the accusation stick mysteriously appear, and Adams is convicted and sentenced to death. The verdict is eventually commuted to a life sentence, but Adams remains behind bars.

The smiling police detectives appear smug and unctuous in suit and tie, while the eyewitnesses lose all credibility as they discredit one another and contradict their courtroom testimony. Morris, however, never scrutinizes a speaker in extreme close-up, and his voice is never heard asking a question. Instead, he punctuates the interviews of various witnesses with odd insert shots that seem to mock the speakers. When David Harris mentions the word *gun*, a rotating catalog illustration of a chrome revolver pops into frame. Star eyewitness Emily Miller confides that she "wanted to be the wife of a detective or be a detective" as we cut to cheap B-movie footage of an old Boston Blackie serial. Macrophotographs of newspaper clippings loom so close the pores of the newsprint are visible. A cutout of a pocket watch sways to and fro as a detective recounts the hypnotic treatments given Wood's partner Turko to jog her memory of the killer's license. Morris even provides lurid clips of exploitation films (*The Student Body* and *Swinging Cheerleaders*), the same films viewed by Harris and Adams at a drive-in movie. In the final scene, wherein Harris all but confesses to the killing, Morris cuts to progressively tighter and revealing shots—of a microcassette recorder (Morris's camera had broken down shortly before the final interview).

Despite Morris's professed admiration for the gritty documentaries of Frederick Wiseman (*Titticut Follies* 1967), his own preference for art over journalism parallels more closely Vertov's subjective techniques. Morris's preoccupation with repetitive circular forms, such as a revolving patrol car light, birds-eye shots of an ashtray, and close-ups of a ticking clock, recall Vertov's eye motif. The palpitating, rhythmic music of Philip Glass is based on circular themes, repeating without resolving; it suggests a mounting inexorable force swirling the characters through a vortex of uncontrollable events.

The stylized reenactments, which were shot in Brooklyn and the Bronx rather than Dallas, have the airbrushed neon look of a vintage Hitchcock picture such as *North by Northwest* (1959) or *Vertigo* (1958). A dramatized scene of the shooting from a police detective's account has the policemen twirl in a slow-motion pirouette as he falls to the ground. An actress in an officer's uniform is seen sipping a chocolate malt; as shots ring out she hurls the cup out the window in a slow motion arc. The camera lingers on the creamy ooze in a scene, which suggests an outtake from a Burger King spot. Indeed, the slick gloss of reenactments in *The Thin Blue Line* undercuts the usual semblance of reality normally sought in dramatizations. As Morris points out, "The re-enactments in *The Thin Blue Line* don't purport to tell you what's true, they in fact illustrate lies, they illustrate fantasies. It's one of the perverse aspects of this movie . . . to take people deeper and deeper into the ambiguities of the case."[12] The reenactments of *The Thin Blue Line* demonstrate that the veracity of recalled experience fades as wishful thoughts proliferate. The high-gloss production of these scenes suggests the nebulous movielike quality of memory, as eyewitness testimony becomes more anecdotal than factual.

Predictably, *The Thin Blue Line* has been likened to Akira Kurasawa's *Rashomon* (1953), a film which depicts the trial of an accused rapist and murderer by illustrating and comparing the different accounts of the accused, the rape victim, a passerby, and the divined spirit of the slain husband. Interestingly, many of the stories told by witnesses in *The Thin Blue Line* offer distinctly different versions of the incidents and fit like mismatched pieces of a jigsaw puzzle. Morris, however, takes exception to the *Rashomon* comparison:

If what they mean is that everything is subjective, just thinking something makes it so, I don't believe that for a second. For me there's a fact of the matter, a fact of what happened on the roadway that night someone sat in the driver's seat of that blue compact car, someone pulled the gun from out underneath the seat, someone pulled the trigger, someone shot Robert Wood. And it was either Randall Adams or David Harris. That's the fundamental issue at the center of all this. Is it knowable? Yes it is. We have access to the world out there, we're not just prisoners of our fantasies or dreams. I wanted to make a movie about how truth is difficult to know, not how it's impossible to know.[13]

In December, with the help of evidence revealed in *The Thin Blue Line*, Adams's attorney pressed for a new trial wherein David Harris exonerated Adams and openly confessed, "my finger was on the trigger."[14] In March 1989, responding to mounting pressure, the Texas Court of Criminal Appeals set aside the murder conviction of Randall Dale Adams. *The Thin Blue Line* hero was met by a wide line of reporters as he emerged from jail a free man. Adams, returning to his home in Columbus, Ohio, suddenly found himself a minor celebrity, the subject of news programs and talk shows. Meanwhile in Texas, the case continued to create waves of public outrage, resulting in the dismissal of one Dallas prosecutor and the resignation of two others.

The Thin Blue Line was named best documentary of 1988 by both the New York Critics Circle and the National Society of Film Critics, and turned up on more ten-best film lists than any other motion picture released that year.[15] *The New Yorker* called the film "a trancelike, lyrical rendering . . . as hypnotic as *Vertigo*." Spike Lee, an influential and controversial filmmaker in his own right, acknowledged that it was "the only time I've seen a film take real effect—that got a guy out of jail."[16]

Despite critical acclaim and the fact that it freed an innocent man, *The Thin Blue Line* failed to gain a best documentary nomination by the conservative Academy of Motion Picture Arts and Sciences. "This is a case of the emperor having no clothes," sniffed one academy member, while another observed that "the film was *not* well liked." The film's unique and unorthodox style, with its curious inserts and reenactments, was mentioned as the chief annoyance. "If [Morris] had done a *60 Minutes* documentary with talking heads, film clips, and conventional narration, they would have nominated it," noted film critic Ebert.[17]

Unfortunately for Morris, a preference for personal moviemaking over journalistic documentary technique would cause him problems again. Though prosecuting attorney Doug Mulder was immune from prosecution for his role in Adams's case, Errol Morris was not. In May 1989, *The Thin Blue Line* saga took another turn when Adams's attorney fired off a vitriolic letter to Morris, demanding return of the rights to Adams's story and $60,000 payment. In 1986, Adams had signed a release granting Morris the right to portray Adams's story. In return, Morris agreed to pay him $10 for a documentary, $40,000 for a television movie, and $60,000 for a feature film. Adams's claim hinged on his contention that the $10 payment, which Morris asserted was sent via courier, never arrived. Even Morris's insistence that his films be considered "movies" rather than "documentaries" perversely undermined his own case. Citing its many reenactments, slick production values, and theatrical release in movie theaters, Adams's attorney called *The Thin Blue Line* a dramatic feature, demanding $60,000 for his client. The lawsuit was eventually settled out of court, but left hard feelings between Adams and Morris, and left them no longer on speaking terms.

Errol Morris won a MacArthur Foundation grant in 1989, and went on to direct the feature film *The Dark Wind*, based on Tony Hillerman's novel. The picture was beset with problems as the target of Native American protests, and never found theatrical release in the United States. Morris washed his hands of the project and and went on to make *A Brief History of Time*, nominally based upon Newton scholar Stephen Hawking's best-selling book about theoretical physics and the origin of the universe. The film, largely a biography of Hawking, played to mixed reviews; some critics were disappointed by the film's overly reverential stance, pointing out that the filmmaker had failed to interview key witnesses, including a woman reputed to be Hawking's former mistress. Others pointed out that the overall seriousness of the piece was compromised by the inclusion of Morris's characteristically frivolous imagery, particularly a shot of a chicken strutting about the cosmos (a scene Hawking himself disliked).[18]

Morris has recently augmented his income producing commercials for 7-11, and American Express. Nonetheless, he has not abandoned his fond themes of offbeat Americana he once proposed (for which he was turned down) as a series for PBS, which he called *Oddballs, One-Shots and Curiosities*. In early 1995, he told a reporter of his hopes of launching a television series he had dreamed up called "The Interrotron Stories," conceived on interviews "based around me and my perspective," using a device that allows an interviewer's face to be superimposed directly in front of the camera lens. Morris may never make another film that approaches *The Thin Blue Line*. No matter—clients have been pursuing him avidly for the signature style of his "Interrotron" technique, and he stays busy with his commercial production company, which he calls "my real MacArthur."[19]

NOTES

1. Errol Morris, interview. Byron Leonard, "Errol Morris: Listening to Our Stories," *Facets* catalog, Number 9, p. 4.

2. Errol Morris, interview. *Cineaste* 17, no. 1 (1989), p. 16.

3. Katherine Dieckmann, "Private Eye," *American Film*, January-February 1989, p. 36.

4. Ibid., "Private Eye," pp. 36–38.

5. Mark Singer, "Predilections," *The New Yorker*, September 6, 1988, p. 43.

6. Singer, "Predilections," pp. 47–48.

7. Singer, "Predilections," pp. 47–48.

8. Errol Morris, interview. *POV*, Public Broadcasting System, KCET, Los Angeles, September 2, 1988.

9. Dieckmann, "Private Eye," p. 33.

10. Singer, "Predilections," p. 50.

11. Dieckmann, "Private Eye," p. 36.

12. Errol Morris, interview. Bill Moyers, *American Playhouse*, Public Broadcasting System, KCET, Los Angeles, April 29, 1989.

13. Moyers, *American Playhouse*, April 29, 1989.

14. Margaret Carlson, reported by Lianne Hart/Columbus, "Recrossing *The Thin Blue Line*: Randall Adams is Free of Everything but the Media," *Time*, April 3, 1989, p. 23.

15. Singer, "Predilections," p. 70.

16. David Handelman, "Insight to Riot: Director Spike Lee's *Do the Right Thing* Takes a Provocative Look at Race Relations," *Rolling Stone*, July 13, 1989, p. 75.

17. Jack Mathews, "*The Thin Blue Line*: Justice For All?" *Los Angeles Times*, March 12, 1989, p. E7.

18. Morris remarked that he kept the shot in the film "simply because I felt it was the first and only opportunity I would have to put a chicken in the stars, and I thought I should avail myself of the opportunity while I had the chance." Errol Morris, interview. *Interview*, October 27, 1993, p. 140.

19. Shawn Rosenheim, "Trying to Get a Fact-Fiction Mix on the Air," *New York Times*, May 4, 1994, C1.

CHAPTER 10

Louisiana Story:
sex, lies, and videotape
(1989)

USA: R

35mm Color

Directed by Steven Soderbergh

Cast in credits order:

James Spader. . . . . Graham

Andie MacDowell. . . . . Ann

Peter Gallagher. . . . . John

Laura San Giacomo. . . . . Cynthia

Ron Vawter. . . . . Therapist

Steven Brill. . . . . Barfly

Alexandra Root. . . . . Woman on Tape

Earl T. Taylor. . . . . Landlord

David Foil. . . . . John's Colleague

Cinematography by Walt Lloyd

Music by Cliff Martinez

Written by

Steven Soderbergh

Steven Soderbergh

Production designed by Joanne Schmidt

Costume design by James Ryder

Produced by

   John Hardy

   Robert Newmyer

> You used to have waves of talent, whether it was the *Nouvelle Vague* from France in the '60s or when you had the young Bogdanovich, Scorsese and Coppola all at once in the 70s. Now, there hasn't been a wave in so long that Steven Soderbergh became a one-man wave, and everyone went disproportionately crazy.
>
> Lem Dobbs, Screenwriter[1]

Of the films discussed herein, Steven Soderbergh's *sex, lies, and videotape* is perhaps the most unusual, closer in form and content to a small Hollywood film of the early 1970s than a no-budget film of the 1980s. Unlike many other independent films, *sex, lies* was not shot on 16mm or in black-and-white, and it included actors who, if not yet stars, were already familiar to moviegoers from films such as *Greystoke: The Legend of Tarzan, Lord of the Apes, Less than Zero*, and *Summer Lovers*. It was not truly a low-budget film by independent standards, having cost more than $1 million to make. Its director even had Hollywood agent. This was the film, however, that would put the Sundance (*nee* U.S.) Film Festival on the map, take the Cannes Film Festival by storm, and ultimately pull in more than $25 million in the United States alone—more revenue than *She's Gotta Have It, Stranger Than Paradise,* and *Blood Simple* combined. This was the independent film that beat the odds and went mainstream, fueling the dreams of indie wannabes across the nation.

An outsider from the start, Steven Soderbergh was born far from the entertainment meccas of Los Angeles and New York, in the southern city of Baton Rouge, Louisiana. When Soderbergh was thirteen, his father, a professor at Louisiana State University, enrolled him in an animation course. Soderbergh exhibited a talent for drawing, but found the amount of artwork required for even short sequences boring and tedious. "I quickly gravitated toward grabbing the Nizo [a high-quality German-made Super-8 movie camera] and shooting live action,"[2] he later recalled. Appropriately, he audited a live-action Super-8 filmmaking class taught by Michael McCallum, which comprised the sum total of his formal education in film. In an interview with *Rolling Stone's* Terri Minsky, he recalled that the primary rule was "You can do anything you want, so long as you don't shoot footage at the zoo and then put that Simon and Garfunkel song to it."[3]

Between 1977 and 1979, Soderbergh made four short films, beginning with an ExLax commercial accompanied by the Doobie Brothers tune "It Keeps You Running," described as "mostly an excuse to use camera angles and editing."[4] At fifteen, he completed a twenty-minute homage to *Taxi Driver* and *The Conversation* entitled *Janitor*. Soderbergh later dismissed the piece, but acknowledged that it taught him the pitfalls of making films about other movies. "I began to realize that the films I had made revealed only my interest in other films and nothing about myself. My friends' films tended to be experimental in nature but very personal, and I decided to explore this area as well."[5] In 1980 he made the highly personal *Skoal*, a black-and-white experimental collage based on his last year of high school that Soderbergh still recalls as one of his more memorable works.

Graduating from high school at age seventeen, Soderbergh went to live with his sister in San Francisco, where he pursued some fruitless industry "contacts" and began writing his first feature-length script. His former LSU instructor McCallum hired him as an editing assistant on the NBC television show *Games People Play*. Although the show eventually was cancelled, Soderbergh stayed in Los Angeles and worked a number of odd jobs: holding cue cards, keeping game-show scoreboards, and editing for the cable television firm Showtime.

Discouraged and disillusioned with Tinseltown, Soderbergh returned to Baton Rouge. Almost immediately, he started another film with money earned as a still photographer for a local commercial director. This work, a thirteen-minute Richard Lesteresque autobiographical short entitled *Rapid Eye Movement*, was inspired by his tribulations in Hollywood. At the same time, Soderbergh took a new job, working for $70 a week as a coin changer in a video game arcade. Soderbergh eventually found a job at a video production house, where he spent two and a half years honing his production and postproduction skills. Meanwhile, he wrote several screenplays and tried to find financial backing for them.

A friend at Showtime recommended Soderbergh to members of the rock group Yes, who were looking for someone to direct a rockumentary documenting their upcoming concert tour. The musicians, looking for an unknown, affordable director, hired Soderbergh upon seeing *Rapid Eye Movement* and a video he had shot of a New Orleans band. The resulting hour-long music video, entitled *90125*, was eventually nominated for a Grammy award—the music-industry equivalent of an Oscar. With these credentials and a draft of an original screenplay, *Crosstalk*, Soderbergh found both an agent and screenwriting assignments (though the projects he worked on were never made).[6]

In the fall of 1986, Soderbergh used some of the money he earned from these projects to make another short. The film, *Winston*, shot over two weekends with a small group of friends and $7,500, presaged the themes of sexual deception and alienation that would emerge fully realized in *sex, lies, and videotape* two years later. Unlike many other young filmmakers who favored style over substance, Soderbergh "tried to keep in mind a certain kind of American film that I really responded to, things like *The Last Picture Show* and *Five Easy Pieces* and *Carnal Knowledge*, films that I felt were just great films: I didn't want to throw the camera around a lot and I wanted to let the performances take priority."[7]

Soderbergh vowed to return to Hollywood, and in late 1987 drove from Louisiana back to the West Coast. Along the way, he devoted himself to his new project, which took him all of eight days to write—in his parents' spare bedroom, on the road, and crashed out on the couch of a friend. The script, *sex, lies and videotape*, seemed too personal to Soderbergh, however, who told interviewer Terri Minsky "I didn't know if anybody would read it. I didn't know if my agent would say, 'I can't send this out.' "[8]

Soderbergh has described his film as having its origins in a year in his life when he was "behaving badly." Investors were reportedly uneasy with the title—they didn't find the words *sex* or *lies* objectionable, but some thought the term *videotape* could mislead potential moviegoers into thinking that the film was actually *shot* using the comparatively low-quality electronic medium.

The film opens with a shot of scrolling blacktop photographed from the hood of a moving automobile over Leo Kottke–type guitar picking. We see Graham in the driver's seat of a convertible from a low angle. This is crosscut with an interior livingroom scene where Ann Mullaney tells her therapist about an obsessive concern she has had about the global accumulation of garbage. The car pulls up beside Ray's Bait Shop and Gas, and Graham finds himself shaving in the restroom.

In a high-rise office with a river view, Ann's husband, John, a successful young attorney, confides to a friend over the telephone his itchiness about being married. Ann's voiceover continues, explaining her concern about her relationship with John, as we see John arriving with a small potted plant at the studio-home of Cynthia, a sexy brunette (and sister of Ann). John and Cynthia romp throughout the house and onto the bed.

Back in her livingroom, the therapist embarrasses Ann with questions about whether or not she masturbates, an act she considers "stupid." Ann is also anxious and uneasy about a high school friend John has invited to visit. Meanwhile, John and Cynthia quickly conclude their lovemaking, prompting Cynthia's sarcastic remark, "I only get one today? Gosh, how exciting." John dresses while explaining that his houseguest will necessitate postponing further trysts. Cynthia fiendishly suggests they do it in John's home, and expresses wistful curiosity about the mysterious visitor.

Graham, dressed head-to-toe in black, pulls up to the Mullaney residence, extinguishes his smoke in a butt-choked dashboard ashtray, and retrieves his black jacket from the trunk (which contains a box of videocassettes and a camcorder). A flustered Ann invites him in, and the two converse awkwardly in the expansive livingroom, as the camera creeps imperceptibly throughout intercuts of closeups and reverse shots. The conversation reveals Graham's quirky, irreverent character, and the nervous, neurotic personality of Ann.

That evening, the three have dinner in an elegant dining room decorated in somber blacks, while John displays his characteristic boorishness in blunt chides about Graham's clothing. Ann tells Graham a little about her sister Cynthia ("she's an extrovert . . . she's loud") and recommends possible apartments to him. Graham tells of his reluctance to clutter his lifestyle with more than one key on his ring, and offers his conception of the two lowest forms of human life: liars and lawyers.

The next day Cynthia gets a call from John inviting her over to the house. "You are scum—I'll be there," she replies with barely concealed glee. Across town, a landlord shows Ann and Graham a modest apartment, which Graham agrees to let. Cynthia, wearing a black hat, lets herself into John's bedroom, where he waits naked and supine, holding a large potted vine over his private parts. "Is this for me?" she asks as she lifts the gift, and looking down, asks innocently, "Is that for me?"

"Can I tell you something personal?" a female voice asks. In a cafe, Ann reveals to Graham her uninterest in sex. Graham, in turn, confides to her that he is impotent in the "presence of others." They talk about psychotherapy, while Ann nervously toys with her wine glass. Meanwhile, Cynthia slips out the front door of the Mullaney house.

That night, Ann lies awake in bed beside John, and gets up and creeps upstairs to the guest room to glimpse the blue-lit form of sleeping Graham. His eyes are open—he knows he's being looked in upon. We hear a rare moment of soft ambient music.

In the therapist's house, Ann speaks with hushed wonder about Graham. Ann also talks to her sister about Graham, when they visit together later in the day. Cynthia supposes that, given a chance to meet him, Graham might be sexually attracted to her. Ann doesn't want her sister to meet him, lest she corrupt the ethereal Graham. Cynthia searches about for a lost pearl earring, cursing.

"What is the most unusual location you've ever masturbated in?" asks Graham's disembodied voice over the grainy video closeup of a young woman in profile. Graham sits in a chair, caressing himself as he gazes at the screen, while the woman describes an autoerotic episode that she secretly enjoyed during a flight on a crowded airliner. A knock at the door announces the intrusion of Ann, interrupting the viewing. Nonplused but amiable, Graham invites her in to his new apartment and fixes iced tea, while Ann curiously peruses his videotape collection. "Why do these tapes all have women's names on them?" she asks naively. When Graham reveals the sexual content of the tapes, Ann becomes uneasy and quickly leaves.

Back at home, Ann makes an urgent phone call warning Cynthia to avoid Graham. This only piques Cynthia's curiosity. When John calls with a proposition, she refuses him and goes to find out about Graham for herself. She introduces herself to the surprised Graham, and he gets around to asking her to sit for a video interview. Intrigued, she agrees and recalls the first time she saw a penis. The next shot makes a temporal leap as Cynthia gives Graham one long glance before leaving his apartment in sheepish silence.

Aroused from her time spent with Graham, Cynthia calls John at work and urges him to come over and make love to her immediately.

"Should I take my skirt off?" asks Cynthia's video image on Graham's television screen. A naked Graham watches the video, then looks away lost in thought; on the tape, Cynthia asks if he thinks she is pretty. As Cynthia's voice continues, telling about John and Ann, ethereal electronic music wafts through the background.

In Cynthia's bedroom, a zoom in–dolly back shot reveals Cynthia in the throes of sex, naked and climaxing, then falling beside the perspiring John in an oddly composed shot wherein the recumbent lovers appear to be standing up. "You can go now," she dismisses him. Later, in a telephone conversation, Cynthia tells an incredulous and indignant Ann all about her interview, suggesting that she masturbated naked before Graham's camera.

Upbeat industrial rock music plays as Ann walks along a graffiti-scarred wall to the dimly lit tavern where Cynthia works as a barmaid. In the bar, the two women discuss a sundress Ann has bought for their mother, as a drolly obnoxious drunk tries to include himself in the conversation.

At night, Ann finds herself sleepless. Freeing herself from John's smothering embrace, she sits in a chair facing him and pointedly asks if he is "having an affair." John coarsely denies it, but Ann does not appear satisfied with his answer; she accuses him of sleeping with Cynthia. John cautions her not to judge him unless she has "evidence" and feigns hurt feelings. Ann relents and comes to bed.

In Cynthia's scarlet bedroom the next day, John is appalled to hear about her video interview with Graham. "Did you have to masturbate in front of him?" he asks. "Those tapes could show up anywhere," he worries. While Ann obsessively tidies the house, she finds Cynthia's pearl earring jamming in her vacuum cleaner. Enraged, she quickly changes clothes and hops in the car, putting her hands over ears to shield them from the din of car alarms and other noise; when she pulls her hands away and all is quiet, she finds herself at Graham's.

Inside the apartment, Graham confesses he knew of John's infidelity. Ann offers to sit for one of Graham's interviews, an offer that he initially refuses.

Ann is persistent, however, and he prepares to interview. A brief cut to black is followed by an establishing shot of the Mullaney house. The soft music reemerges together with the sound of birds as Ann lies back, her hair down, on the sofa. Graham, beside her, looks into her eyes. Ann returns home and tells John that she "wants out of this marriage." John is stunned when he learns that she has come from Graham's. He demands, "Did you make one of these goddamned videotapes?"

Furious, John drives to Graham's and bursts in on the sleeping man, looking for the incriminating tapes. He punches Graham and ejects him forcibly from the apartment, locking him out. Finding the videotape of Ann, he inserts it in the player and sits down to watch. Ominous, throbbing music plays in the background. The interview begins.

> **GRAHAM:** Do you have sex?
>
> **ANN:** Not very often, no.
>
> **GRAHAM:** When you do, who usually initiates it?
>
> **ANN:** He does.
>
> **GRAHAM:** Is the sex satisfying?
>
> **ANN:** I don't know, I don't know what you mean.
>
> **GRAHAM:** Do you have orgasms?
>
> **ANN:** I don't think so.

John rubs his face in chagrin, as he watches his wife's confession on the screen.

> **GRAHAM:** Have you ever thought about having sex with someone other than your husband?
>
> **ANN:** I've thought about it.

A flashback takes us to the real-time scene as it plays between Ann and Graham, leaving the voyeurism of the contrasty, grainy tape for the warmth and intimacy of the scene itself. The interviewee has become the interviewer.

> **ANN:** Can you give a woman an orgasm? Could you do that for me? You said you weren't always impotent. What happened, was it so bad it turned you off?

Graham explains how he came to be impotent, of his history as a pathological liar. He lets slip the name of a former lover named Elizabeth. He confesses to moving back to Baton Rouge to realize a "sense of closure."

Ann interrogates Graham relentlessly, picking up the camera to confront him:

> **ANN:** Is this what you would be the rest of your life? Why are you doing this to yourself?
>
> **GRAHAM:** I look around here in this town and I see John, and Cynthia, and you, and I feel comparatively healthy.
>
> **ANN:** You've got a problem.
>
> **GRAHAM:** You're right. I've got a lot of problems. But they belong to me.

Ann counters, "I didn't want to be a part of your problem, but I am. I'm leaving my husband. . . . You've had an effect on my life."

Graham sits staring out the window, while Ann comes up behind him, caressing him. She rests his head on the sofa and lifts his hand to caress her face, enjoying his touch. Graham looks up at her, and she descends to kiss him tenderly. He rises, crosses the room, and shuts the camcorder off.

The tape ends, the television screen a flurry of snow and noise. John rises from the chair and leaves the house. In a final low blow, he stops to tell Graham that he has "fucked" Elizabeth, and could say no more. Graham comes back into the apartment and in an important change of character, smashes all the cassettes, pulling out the tapes and leaving them broken in a mass on the floor.

Black screen. John talks to a client about balancing work with a failed marriage. A voice on the other end of the phone informs John that the client he has repeatedly put off has sought legal council elsewhere. Over the intercom, his secretary tells him that the boss would like to see him immediately. John bids the client goodbye and slams his fist down on the desk, cursing.

Ann brings in a potted plant to the Bayou tavern as a birthday present for Cynthia. Laid-back electronic music with a beat lopes along in the background. Ann appears confident, unperturbed, while Cynthia is uncharacteristically sheepish. "Can I call you?" she asks Ann.

Ann joins Graham, sitting on the porch of his apartment. He caresses her arm. "I think it's going to rain," Ann says. Graham looks up with a smile: "It is raining."

Soderbergh finished the postproduction on *sex, lies* barely in time for the 1989 U.S. (now Sundance) Film Festival in Park City, Utah. He filled his days at the festival as a volunteer, at one point chauffeuring Jody Foster and Beth Henley to film screenings. Each successive screening of his film was more crowded and chaotic than the previous one. In the last days of the festival, Soderbergh remembers being assured by scores of persons, "You're gonna win!" Indeed, when it was all over, *sex, lies, and videotape* had created a popular sensation, winning Sundance's Dramatic Competition Audience Award.

Soderbergh was inundated with offers from all the independent and several of the major distributors. He ultimately accepted a previously unthinkable deal from Miramax Films: $1 million upfront for distribution rights, $1 million for advertising, and a healthy percentage of the gross. He conducted more than 350 interviews as a result of the film's success, one of which he came to regret for disparaging producers Jerry Bruckheimer and Don Simpson as "slime, just barely passing for humans."[9]

But the best was yet to come. It had been only seven years since Susan Seidelman's *Smithereens* became the first American independent feature film to make the main competition at Cannes. Since that time, several independents, including Jarmusch and Lee, had won awards such as Camera d'Or for best first feature. Soderbergh, however, was the first of them to take the festival's highest award, the Palme d'Or; James Spader took the prize for Best Actor. Accepting his award, Soderbergh remarked prophetically to the crowd, "I guess it's all downhill from here."[10] Not everyone was pleased. Soderbergh's coup drew the disapproval of fellow competitor Spike Lee, whose *Do the Right Thing* garnered no awards. In a characteristic display of poor sportsmanship, the peevish Lee groused, "We were robbed." Lee's racially charged film ultimately galvanized many critics, but *sex, lies, and videotape* broke new ground and went on to gross over $35 million in domestic ticket sales alone.

Critics were mostly enthusiastic about *sex, lies, and videotape*. Many found it reminiscent of French director Eric Rohmer's "moral tales," such as *Chloe in the Afternoon*, *Claire's Knee*, and *Pauline at the Beach*, in its delightfully dense conversational technique. But the film's true precursors are the small films that blossomed during the American cinematic renaissance of the late 1960s and early 1970s—films that depicted ordinary people grappling with problems of relationships and interpersonal communications. Looking back at his feature debut triumph, Soderbergh observed wistfully:

> *sex, lies* I think was a fluke. I think it's being used as a benchmark in a financial sense and I think that's a mistake. Now that it appears that there might be money to be made from independent-type films, there's certainly more people who are looking toward that end, not necessarily on the filmmaking side but on the distributor side and on the producer side. They're doing it because they think there's money to be made doing that and that's why they're doing it. It's not because of some overriding belief in film as art.[11]

Soderbergh was right. His first feature had raised the stakes considerably for independent filmmakers across the nation. The year would see the release of a number of remarkable "independent" films: *Mystery Train, Roger & Me, Do the Right Thing*. With *sex, lies, and videotape*, however, Soderbergh unwittingly created the paradigm by which all subsequent independent films would be measured. The atmosphere at future Sundance festivals would never be the same as new independents jockeyed for latest indie flavor-of-the-year status, and festivalgoers attempted to seek out the next *sex, lies, and videotape*.

NOTES

1. Trip Gabriel, "Steven Soderbergh: The Sequel," *New York Times Biographical Service*, November 1991, p. 1166.

2. Steven Soderbergh, *sex, lies, and videotape* (New York: Harper and Row, 1990), p. 24.

3. Terri Minsky, "Hot Phenom: Hollywood Makes a Big Deal Over Steven Soderbergh's *sex, lies, and videotape*," *Rolling Stone*, May 18, 1989, p. 81.

4. Minsky, "Hot Phenom," pp. 85–86.

5. Soderbergh, *sex, lies, and videotape*, p. 140.

6. Minsky, "Hot Phenom," p. 87.

7. Steven Soderbergh, interview. *The Criterion Collection: sex, lies, and videotape* (Santa Monica, CA: Voyager, 1990).

8. Minsky, "Hot Phenom," p. 87.

9. Katherine Deickmann, "Liar, Liar, Pants on Fire: Steve Soderbergh Comes Clean," *Village Voice*, August 8, 1989, p. 32. Soderbergh was reportedly mortified to see his indiscretion in print, noting that his comments were based on an article he had read in *Esquire* magazine. He subsequently recanted in a letter to the editor and offered a personal apology to the producers.

10. "Views from the Edge,"*American Cinema*, Public Broadcasting System, Los Angeles: KCET, April 30, 1995.

11. Ibid.

CHAPTER 11

Rust Belt Requiem: *Roger & Me*
(1989)

USA: R

16mm Color

Written, Produced, and Directed by Michael Moore

Associate Producer Wendy Stanzler

Edited by
  Wendy Stanzler
  Jennifer Beman
Camera by
  Christopher Beaver
  John Prusak
  Kevin Rafferty
  Bruce Schermer
Sound by Judy Irving

> Flint is a microcosm of what's going on in the country. Coming to your town soon . . . and I don't mean the movie. *Roger & Me* is an attempt to get America to pay attention to the face behind the corporations, to pull back the curtain—just as they did in *The Wizard of Oz*.
> Michael Moore[1]

1989 was a banner year for independent filmmakers, a resounding climax to a decade-long crescendo of off-Hollywood *auteur* filmmaking. Early that spring, Errol Morris's *The Thin Blue Line* had whipped up considerable public outcry and hastened the release of a wrongly accused man from a Texas prison. Later in May, the Cannes Film Festival was dominated by independents, led by the mighty triumvirate of Steven Soderbergh's *sex, lies, and videotape*, Jim Jarmusch's *Mystery Train*, and Spike Lee's *Do the Right Thing*.

As summer drew to a close, a new and even more unlikely independent feature was suddenly winning over audiences at the Toronto and New York film festivals. Most baffling was the subject of film: a nonfiction examination of the events leading up to massive General Motors layoffs that devastated the industrial city of Flint, Michigan, in the eighties—hardly an entertaining topic. What made the film an unqualified triumph, however, was the unusual sardonic and ironical wit of its maker, an unemployed magazine editor named Michael Moore. Moore presented various Flint calamities and characters as he goes about his own improbable quest to bring GM's chairman Roger Smith to the ravaged city. He wants Smith to see the consequences of his decision to sack thousands of employees in his hometown.

The idea of examining a serious subject through a humorous personal odyssey was not new. Ross McElwee did much the same thing in his rambling *Sherman's March*, an amusing self-portrait disguised as a historical documentary that had more to do with McElwee's problematic lovelife than it did with any event of the American Civil War. *Roger & Me's* satirical use of quaint archival film material to enliven stuffy or somber subject matter is familiar to those who had seen *The Atomic Cafe* or *The Thin Blue Line*. What is different about *Roger & Me* is the personality of its tireless crusader, Michael Moore himself. His David Letterman-meets-Mike Wallace style won him a broad audience ready to snicker in righteous indignation at the arrogance and neglect of a faceless corporation.

Michael Moore was born in 1954, one year before the General Motors fifty-year anniversary celebrations in Flint depicted at the beginning of *Roger & Me*. A social activist from the age of sixteen, he presented a slide show, for his Eagle Scout project, exposing the worst polluters of his hometown, Davison (a suburb of Flint). Raised Roman Catholic, he enrolled in a Berrigan-order seminary intending to become involved as a political activist, but he left the enclave at the brothers' request. He was happy to go, and recalls wistfully that "in 1968 a lot of important stuff was going on. And I was in a seminary."[2]

Upon returning to Davison High School, Moore excelled in debate and gravitated to student government issues. Early on, he developed a penchant for satirizing his hometown friends and neighbors, as evidenced by a play he wrote for the high school. "It was a religious theme and it ended when Christ comes down off the cross and is nailed back up," he observes. "The people who nailed Christ back up were modeled on people in my home town. They could recognize themselves."³ Upon graduating, Moore's former high school government teacher encouraged him to run for a seat on the Flint school board; Moore, following his personal principles, later returned the favor by lobbying for the instructor's ouster. Townspeople sought Moore's recall from the board, a move that he fought and defeated. Moore helped start a teen crisis center that became embroiled in lawsuits and gradually turned into offices for the muckraking newspaper he founded in 1979, *The Flint Voice*. He was also known for hosting a weekly radio show, *Radio Free Flint*, and for organizing numerous antinuclear protests. *The Voice* made little money but numerous enemies among local authorities with its pointed investigative articles. Moore soon went statewide with the newspaper, changing its name to *The Michigan Voice*. Shortly thereafter, he closed down the operation to take an editing post with left-leaning magazine *Mother Jones* in San Francisco.

As Moore notes in *Roger & Me*, he did not adjust well to life in the Bay Area. *Jones* owner Adam Hochschild dismissed him after five months, citing Moore's inability to get along with others—read: his superiors. Moore claimed the experience so depressed him that he stayed in bed for days, developing the beginnings of what turned out to be a severe weight problem. Moore eventually filed a wrongful termination suit against *Mother Jones* for $2 million.

Returning to Flint, Moore resolved to make a film about his hometown. His inspiration drew from an irreverent documentary spoofing the atomic age sensibilities of the 1940s and 1950s, called *The Atomic Cafe*. It was a compilation film, edited from bits of vintage instructional film and newsreel footage of the day and set to whimsical music and incongruous voiceovers from the period. Moore called upon the film's director Kevin Rafferty to give him a week-long crash course on filmmaking in preparation for the project that would ultimately consume two and half years of his life and most of his savings.

The film began with a simple premise: "I wanted it to be a comedy; I wanted the narrative thread to be my quest for Roger, but it would only be about 20 percent of the film. I'd take people on tour of my hometown, of what had happened to it over the years."⁴ Moore poured the $58,000 settlement he received from the *Mother Jones* lawsuit into the production, along with the proceeds from the sale of his house and *The Michigan Voice*, and the advance he received from Doubleday for an as-yet-unwritten book about Flint. After exhausting those funds, Moore managed to raise an additional $20,000 holding weekly bingo games in his hometown.

Roger & Me begins with a narration by Moore, touching upon his early life and establishing the comedic, idiosyncratic, and often self-important tone of the film in first person voiceover:

I was kind of a strange child. My parents knew early on that something must have been wrong with me. I crawled backwards until I was two, but had Kennedy's inaugural address memorized by the time I was six. It all began when my mother didn't show up for my first birthday party because she was having my sister. My dad tried to cheer me up by letting me eat the whole cake. I knew then there had to be more to life than this.

An opening montage of vintage fifties-era clips, including the spectacle of Pat Boone crooning a sanitized rock and roll tune, continues as a backdrop for Moore's wistful reminiscence:

When I was a kid I thought only three people worked for General Motors: Pat Boone, Dinah Shore—and my dad. Our home town of Flint, Michigan was the birthplace of General Motors, the largest corporation in the world. There were more auto factories and auto workers than in any city on earth. . . . We enjoyed a prosperity that working people around the world had never seen before.

Moore continues to wax nostalgic as newsreel film footage depicts General Motors' fiftieth anniversary celebrations, where "the promise of the future is the keynote." Moore fondly remembers his Uncle Laverne, who participated in Flint's historic sit-down strike of 1937, when the UAW was born. Nevertheless, he concludes that: "The assembly line wasn't for me. My heroes were the Flint people who had escaped the life of the factory and got out of Flint. . . . "

We see Moore editing the small *Michigan Voice*, then taking his editing post at *Mother Jones* in San Francisco. Moore sniffs at the Bay Area yuppie environment, nonplussed by the wide array of coffees and deserts available and perturbed at the absence of nondairy creamer. *Jones*'s owner points Moore toward "an investigative report on herbal teas," but Moore prefers to give a column to a laid-off auto worker and puts the worker's picture on the front cover, prompting the magazine's owner to hand Moore his walking papers.

A tongue-in-cheek sentimental forties-era clip of a young soldier's homecoming is followed by a CBS news clip reporting GM's closure of eleven plants employing 30,000 workers. GM CEO Roger Smith announces the closings at a news conference, which is followed by an image of a dynamited GM water tower toppling over. In a voiceover, Moore notes caustically:

He appeared to have a brilliant plan: first, close eleven factories in the US, then open eleven in Mexico where you pay the workers seventy cents an hour. Then, use the money you save by building cars in Mexico to take over companies, preferably high-tech firms and weapons manufacturers. Next, tell the union you're broke and they happily agree to give back a couple billion dollars in wage cuts. You then take that money from the workers and you eliminate your jobs by building more foreign factories. Roger Smith was a true genius.

The camera shows workers leaving the GM truck factory on their last day of employment. Posing as a Toledo TV crew, Moore's unit records the oddly celebratory events of the last day. A member of the management states flatly, "There is nothing out there for them to depend upon for the future." Interviewed auto workers unanimously criticize CEO Roger Smith, while GM spokesman and lobbyist Tom Kaye stands up for the GM policies from the relative serenity of his office.

Getting nowhere by writing and faxing the corporation for an appointment, Moore takes his film crew to GM World Headquarters in Detroit in an effort to interview Roger Smith, ostensibly to take the helmsman back to Flint to show him the consequences of his act. Getting as far as the elevator, Moore is intercepted by company officials who stop him from trying to see Smith. The crew goes back to Flint to witness the closure of more factories, and visits the worker Moore put on the *Mother Jones* cover, now at a local mental health center. The worker tells of an anxiety attack that forced him to walk off his assembly-line job, and describes the irony of hearing bouncy Beach Boys song "Wouldn't It Be Nice" play on the radio as he drove away. On cue, the 1966 hit promptly begins playing on the soundtrack as the camera rolls by gutted houses and boarded-up storefronts. A news report affirms that rats now exceed the human population in Flint by 50,000.

President Ronald Reagan gets involved by taking a select group of unemployed workers out for pizza, advising them to leave Michigan for work in southern states. One of Flint's founding families hires laid-off workers to act as "human statues" to entertain the well-to-do guests at a *Great Gatsby* theme party. Moore interviews a number of the costumed partygoers, who respond defensively to questions about the calamity in Flint. One man insists, "It's a great place to live."

Grim scenes of winter follow, while sheriff's deputy Fred Ross carries out evictions of jobless Flint citizens, a scene followed by shots of the palatial estates of Michigan's posh Grosse Point neighborhood. Moore visits the Grosse Point Yacht Club in his search for Smith, but ends up chatting with the receptionist instead.

Moore visits the local county fair to witness television personality Bob Eubanks conducting a round of his once-popular *Newlywed Game*. In a backstage interview, Eubanks professes to have no knowledge of the present situation in his hometown, and Moore's camera catches him (presumably unawares) telling an offensive ethnic joke.

Next, Moore attends the annual parade honoring the original Flint sit-down strikers. There, he asks the state governor and the UAW president if another sit-down strike is the answer to the current problem. Failing to get answers, Moore even interrogates Miss Michigan, who struggles to respond diplomatically. Her reluctance to take sides proves prudent, as we see her later going on to capture the Miss America crown.

Meanwhile, Fred Ross continues his work, serving another eviction notice. The tenant of one house tries to show Ross the considerable dilapidation of the structure, but is turned out into the street just the same.

Moore attempts to locate Smith at the posh Detroit Athletic Club, but he is rebuffed by an astringent club representative. Segue to a giant revival meeting hosted by a $20,000 speaker, evangelist Robert Schuller, who mouths sanctimonious platitudes to the crowd. Graffiti and other discouraging scrawls on public works ("Assholes drive imports") intermingle with empty billboard slogans ("Flint Works"), as Schuller's sermon drones on: "Just because you've got problems is no excuse to be unhappy."

Moore visits Flint's Star Theater and listens to a choreographer gush about performers Bobby Vinton and Peggy Lee performing in what he terms "Buick City." Anita Bryant belts out songs and sunny banalities. "Today is a new day," she prattles. Pat Boone offers uplifting bromides, and describes his own sweetheart deal as a television spokesman for GM that provides him two Chevrolets a year. Between signing autographs and visiting churches, he suggests Flint's unemployed investigate distributing opportunities with Amway, Inc.

In a private home, a group of women watch as an Amway representative gives a demonstration on "doing colors" to determine a person's most flattering hues; Moore himself consents to a session. At a local Taco Bell, he learns that laid-off workers who found work at the restaurant have been fired for their failure to adapt to the pace of the fast food outlet. Moore then returns to lobbyist Kaye, who suggests that citizens of Flint look to a manufacturer of lint rollers as a model of entrepreneurism and for potential career opportunities.

A makeshift sign on a telephone pole reads: "Rabbits or bunnies, pets or meat." Moore inquires at the door and a slightly unhinged woman explains how she raises, sells, and butchers rabbits as a way to make a living. A young man on the street tells of selling his blood for extra money. Women wail in the wake of a homicide that has left a body lying in the street, while news reporters affirm that Flint now has the highest violent crime rate in America. This depressing news appears to spark an interest in gun ownership. Moore interviews some former auto workers who now work as prison guards; an inmate rants loudly in the background. Cut to four society women on a golf course who praise the town and criticize the "lazy" unemployed.

Deputy Ross evicts another family, and offers his own analysis of why people are having such hard times. A postal worker tells of the huge increase in change-of-address applications filed, as some 82,000 people leave town. An employee for a truck rental company notes the boom in his business as people rent trucks to move out of the area.

To the accompaniment of the *William Tell Overture,* Moore finally tracks down Roger Smith at an awards ceremony in New York City. One of his crew is recognized as a relative of famed consumer advocate and "arch-nemesis" activist Ralph Nader; he is unceremoniously carried out of the building. Moore returns with renewed determination to see Smith at GM headquarters, but is intercepted a second time and refused entry. "Obviously I was getting the big blowoff once again," he grumbles.

Flint meanwhile has become "the unemployment capital of the nation," according to Moore. The city fathers have an idea to inject life into the languishing city, however, with the commission of a new $13 million hotel in hope of spurring an unlikely tourist trade. The hotel attracts few travelers, prompting the city to erect a "marketplace pavilion" and the $100 million AutoWorld—a replica of yesteryear Flint touted as the world's largest indoor theme park—to renovate the downtown area. Within six months the attractions close.

Lobbyist Kaye makes more excuses for GM's lack of responsibility regarding the welfare of Flint while Deputy Ross evicts another tenant. Moore returns to the rabbit woman, who holds a bunny while raving about a recent run-in with health officials, who have given her thirty days to erect a building for butchering her animals. She blithely clubs and kills the rabbit she has been cuddling and hangs it from a tree to dress it.

Townspeople demonstrate publicly when *Money* magazine rates Flint as the least habitable city in the United States; Bruce Springsteen's sentimental "My Hometown" plays over the scene. ABC's *Nightline* has to cancel a live program from Flint City Hall when someone drives off with the broadcaster's remote van—cables and all. The county responds to the growing crime wave by erecting a huge jail to hold Flint's newly convicted criminals. In another bizarre turn, the city holds a "Jailhouse Rock" fund-raiser one night before the prison's opening for patrons who wish to pay $100 for the privilege of spending a night in jail.

In hopes of confronting Smith, Moore impersonates a stockholder and infiltrates a meeting of GM shareholders. When Moore steps up to the microphone, however, Smith recognizes his pursuer and abruptly adjourns the meeting, chuckling with others as he walks offstage.

Two weeks before Christmas, the factory that hosted the historic sit-down strike is slated to close. Despite the UAW's promise of a demonstration to protest the closing, only four demonstrators show up. A GM spokeswoman curtly tells Moore to get off the property.

On Christmas Eve, General Motors hosts a Christmas extravaganza in Detroit while Deputy Ross evicts yet another unfortunate tenant. Smith recites a stuffy Christmas testimonial. In voiceover, the passage he reads from Dickens narrates another family's departure from Flint; they collect their belongings and clear out of their house in a flurry of curses. As the GM festivities conclude, Moore is able finally to confront Smith. He tells him about the many evicted people and elicits a predictably curt response: "I cannot come to Flint. I'm sorry."

As the camera zooms back from a fluttering flag to reveal an abandoned GM building, Moore concludes his film: "Well, I failed to bring Roger to Flint. As we neared the end of the twentieth century, the rich were richer, the poor poorer, and people everywhere had a lot less lint, thanks to the lint rollers made in my hometown. It was truly the dawn of a new era."

Closing titles reveal that GM apologist Tom Kaye was himself laid off, his office closed. Eubanks cracks another off-color joke, the rabbit woman reveals her horrendous plans to study veterinary assistance because, "there's a lot of animals that needs takin' care of," and Pat Boone sings "Happy Birthday to Flint" in Bill Murray fashion as demolition crews topple the walls of a factory.

A final title reads: "This film cannot be shown within the city of Flint. All the movie theaters have closed." In a final slathering of editorial irony, *Roger & Me* ends with this exhortation from Anita Bryant, "And if you decide to go for it, you'll make it."

Moore, trained as a journalist, literally learned the craft of filmmaking while making *Roger & Me*. In one humorous instance, when then-presidential candidate Jesse Jackson agreed to be interviewed for the film, the political hopeful repeatedly told Moore that the sound operator was recording the conversation with the tape recorder knob in the wrong position. Moore ignored Jackson and went ahead with the interview—only to find out there was indeed no sound on the tape. The Jackson interview does not appear in the film.

No sooner did the film emerge than it started to spark tumultuous audience approval and critical accolades. *Roger & Me* set attendance records at Colorado's Telluride Film Festival, was voted "most popular" film in Toronto, and drew a seventeen-minute standing ovation at the New York Film Festival. The film ultimately earned Best Documentary honors from the National Board of Review, National Society of Film Critics, and the Los Angeles Film Critics Association.[5]

Roger & Me kicked off a furious bidding war among distributors, who didn't want to miss another bus after Soderbergh's unexpected success with *sex, lies, and videotape*. Riding a wave of critical adulation, *Roger & Me* then accomplished the unthinkable: a major studio, Warner Brothers, ultimately paid Moore a whopping $3 million to distribute the $260,000 film. The

16mm film went on to gross over $25 million, becoming the most lucrative documentary in motion picture history.[6]

At Moore's insistence, the distributor also agreed to purchase houses for some of the evictees shown in the film, hand out 20,000 free movie tickets for the unemployed citizens, and fund a *Roger & Me* promotional office in Flint. Moore, only partly in jest, also requested that Warner Brothers also ensure that each theater save an empty seat, just in case Roger Smith himself decided to see the film. Accused by some of "going Hollywood" and collaborating with corporate America in his association with the motion picture conglomerate, Moore chuckled in his defense, "I had this terrible nightmare that somehow the revolution would begin, I would be stuck riding around in one of these limousines, and they'd be hauling me out and I'd say, 'no, really, Warners made me, I didn't mean to.' "[7]

Opening nationwide in forty cities, the movie pulled a solid $687,000 in its first weekend. Critics waxed ecstatic over the film's jabs at corporate America floundering in the wake of Reaganomics. In his review for the *New York Times*, Vincent Canby hailed Moore as "an irrepressible new humorist in the tradition of Mark Twain,"[8] while David Denby of *New York* magazine likened him to H. L. Mencken and Sinclair Lewis.[9] Gene Siskel and Roger Ebert both gave glowing reviews and placed the film on their ten-best lists for 1989.

Others weren't so sure. J. Hoberman praised the film but derided its "shameless use of Christmas" and its less-than-subtle irony laid on, he wrote, "with a trowel."[10] Pauline Kael called the film a "piece of gonzo demagoguery" that proffered "leftism as a superior attitude." Kael went a step further and criticized its supporters, attributing its widespread popularity to the belief that "members of the audience can laugh at ordinary working people and still feel that they're taking a politically correct position."[11]

Critics soon found ammunition to back up their unfavorable opinions when it was revealed that certain points in the film didn't jibe with the actual chronology of events. Harlan Jacobson, in particular, mercilessly grilled Moore in a much-discussed *Film Comment* interview, revealing that Moore had played fast and loose with his editing of events leading up to the Flint layoffs. In building dramatic momentum in his film, it appeared that Moore had juggled the sequence of indirectly or unrelated events to suggest causal relationships among them. Many of the scenes that were edited to appear as if they were the direct consequences of GM's raft of layoffs had in fact transpired several years earlier. Jacobson sums it up: "The impression that one has from the movie is that there was a single felling blow, directed at Fisher Plant #1, which cut loose 30,000 people from employment, resulting in immediate and massive devastation to which the local government responded with fantasy projects."[12]

Indeed, the arrival of televangelist Robert Schuller, edited in the film to appear to follow the Smith layoffs, had in fact occurred in 1982. Flint's ill-conceived tourist attractions were not actually opened in 1986 or 1987 as a way to revitalize the city's flagging economy, as the film implies. Rather, the Hyatt Regency Hotel opened in 1982, the theme park AutoWorld opened in mid-1984 (closing six months later),[13] and the Water Street Pavilion opened less than a year after that. Perhaps the most glaring misrepresentation is the depiction of a cavalier Ronald Reagan buying pizza dinner for twelve unemployed workers and telling them to desert the city and seek work in Texas—an event actually shot in 1980 when Reagan was still campaigning for office. It turned out that even the scene's punch line was a misrepresentation: the cash register that purportedly "walked off" during the former California governor's visit had actually disappeared two days earlier.

When these discrepancies in *Roger & Me* came to light, many who originally praised the film now voiced belated reservations. Some pundits like Denby published afterwords to their own earlier reviews. Georgia Brown summed up the feelings of many when she ended her December 26, 1989, *Village Voice* article with the thought: "it's one thing to play fair with Roger Smith and another to play fair with the audience."[14]

The controversy continued to reverberate. In a move that recalled *The Thin Blue Line* flap one year earlier, the Academy of Motion Picture Arts and Sciences snubbed *Roger & Me*, passing it over for a best documentary nomination. One Academy member's criticism of Moore's methodology: "He presented a time continuum which didn't exist, which in my mind is dishonest and unethical."[15]

Moore shrugged off the criticism, even suggesting that his manipulation of real-life events constituted a new cinematic form, the "docu-comedy." He told a reporter that:

> Any time a person comes along and tries to advance an art form to a new phase, he meets resistance from those who consider themselves the keepers of the old flame. Truman Capote was told that *In Cold Blood* wasn't nonfiction. "How could you write it? You weren't there." Yet he helped usher in a new era—the New Journalism.[16]

What disturbed many observers was not the attack on corporate management's treatment of its workers, but what they perceived as Moore's flip, condescending depiction of his working-class peers. Others joined the fray as well. UAW workers picketed the film in Detroit for its purported portrayal of union president Owen Bieber as a GM dupe. The American Humane Society decried the scene of the rabbit slaughter demonstrated by the Rabbit Lady and lobbied for its removal from the film. Ralph Nader demanded repayment of a $30,000 donation he had made to the production before the film became a hit. And after the film showed remarkable earning power at the box office, at least two parties sued Moore for purportedly stealing the ideas for *Roger & Me*. Moore was undoubtedly wondering which he had become: this year's pet or simply meat?

After a six-month promotional tour, Moore settled into his new office in the Warner Brothers building in New York to work on a script about the Holocaust.[17] In the meantime Moore produced a short video sequel to *Roger & Me* entitled *Pets or Meat*, where he revisits some of the folks seen in his first movie. The program, made for $55,000, was shown on PBS in 1991. When the Gulf War broke out, he focused on a *Dr. Strangelove*–style black comedy wherein the U.S. government, looking for an adversary to take the Soviet Union's place in the new world order, conspires with a major defense firm to declare war on Canada. Warner Brothers ultimately passed on the project, but Moore found funding through Phillips-owned Propaganda Films. The film, entitled *Canadian Bacon*, wrapped shooting early in 1994 with John Candy in the leading role (he passed away shortly thereafter). In May 1995, Moore took the film to Cannes, where he found a chilly reception. The film was released later that summer, but lacking critical plaudits or popular interest, it sank without a trace.

In the meantime, Moore created a six-episode "reality" series entitled *TV Nation*, which took *Roger & Me*'s jocular crusader to various parts of the globe to investigate some of modern industry's more ironic abuses. The series ran two summer seasons, but the show failed to be renewed by NBC.

Looking back on his first film, Moore acknowledges wistfully that "in the bigger picture, the problem isn't Roger Smith. The problem isn't General Motors. The problem is that we have an economic system in this country that's unfair and unjust and not democratic."[18] Ultimately an indictment of traditional American optimism and its failure in the face of a profound economic disaster, *Roger & Me* may in fact be a nostalgic homage to industrial halcyon days that Americans may never again enjoy.

Despite its gloomy view of the American way of life, the film brought along inspiring proof that a nobody could come out of nowhere to make a wildly successful 16mm feature film, free of the Hollywood establishment, and go on to capture the imaginations (and dollars) of millions. In retrospect, its success is easy to understand. This portrait of the American dream gone sour paradoxically turned out to fulfill that dream for its maker, and gave audiences a success story they wanted to see as the fast-spending 1980s crashed to a close.

With the 1990s came an era of profound recession, as the Persian Gulf War and its aftermath played havoc with the global economy, but new independent filmmakers were emerging to make ever more lucrative deals. At the 1991 Sundance Festival awards ceremony, Moore was booed roundly when he attempted to enlist John Sayles to rally the audience and condemn

U.S. involvement in the ongoing Persian Gulf War. Alternative film buffs and wheeler-dealers may have welcomed Moore's investigative comedy routine in *Roger & Me*, but they wanted no part of his left-wing politics now. After all, there were deals to be made. Even as video markets dried up and distribution opportunities grew tighter, a new brood of lucrative no-budget independent films was beginning to emerge: *Metropolitan, Slacker, El Mariachi, Clerks,* and others. As Moore prophesized in his parting remark from *Roger & Me*, it was—for independent filmmakers anyway—"the dawning of a new era."

NOTES

1. Michael Moore, interview. Elaine Dutka, "Tyro in the Land of the Titans," *Los Angeles Times*, November 4, 1989, p. F10.

2. Michael Moore, interview. Jim Emerson, "Moore's Dream & *Roger & Me*," *Orange County Register*, January 2, 1990, p. F5.

3. Michael Moore, interview. John Marchese, "Me: The Continuing Adventures of Michael Moore," *Esquire*, January 1993, pp. 45–46.

4. Emerson, "Moore's Dream & *Roger & Me*," p. F5.

5. Renee Tajima, "The Perils of Popularity," *The Independent*, June 1990, p. 30.

6. Excluding concert films such as *Woodstock* (the Director of *Woodstock*, 1969).

7. Michael Moore, interview. *ABC Primetime Live*, American Broadcasting Company, KABC, Los Angeles, Janauary 2, 1990.

8. Vincent Canby, "Rejoice! It's Independents' Day," *New York Times*, October 8, 1989, p. B1.

9. David Denby, *New York*, December 18, 1989, p. 102.

10. J. Hoberman, *Village Voice*, October 3, 1989, p. 62.

11. *The New Yorker*, December 1989, p. 84.

12. In an incident that recalled Moore's own dismissal from *Mother Jones*, Jacobson was reportedly fired from the magazine after controversy heated up over both Moore's documentary techniques and Jacobson's own railing in the article, where, among other things, he compared Moore's lack of truthfulness to Lyndon B. Johnson's deceptions surrounding the Gulf of Tonkin incident in the mid-1960s. Jacobson maintained that the Film Society of Lincoln Center dismissed him because they liked the film and were displeased with the critical tone of the article. The society's director, Joanne Koch, denied the accusation, noting that the board had decided it was time to take the magazine in a new direction. Tajima, "Perils of Popularity," p. 30.

13. Ironically, the amusement park reopened for six weeks to coincide with the premiere of *Roger & Me* in Flint (an event deemed impossible in the final credits of the film).

14. Geroge Brown, *Village Voice*, December 26, 1989, p. 102.

15. Elaine Dutka, "Will Controversy Cost *Roger* an Oscar?," *Los Angeles Times*, January 17, 1990, p. F1.

16. Dutka, "Tyro in the Land of the Titans," p. F10.

17. The script has yet to be produced.

18. Emerson, "Moore's Dream & *Roger & Me*," p. F5.

Bibliography

Interview with Michael Moore. *ABC Primetime Live*, American Broadcasting Corp., KABC, Los Angeles, December 21, 1989.

Andrew, Geoff. *The Film Handbook*. Boston: G. K. Hall, 1989.

Ansen, David. Review of *Blood Simple*. *Newsweek*, January 21, 1985: 74.

————. Review of *sex, lies, and videotape*. *Newsweek*, August 7, 1989: 61.

————. Review of *Stranger Than Paradise*. *Newsweek*, October 8, 1984: 87.

————. "Hollywood Goes Independent." *Newsweek*, April 6, 1987: 64–66.

Arrington, Carol. "Film's Avant-Guardian." *Rolling Stone*, March 22, 1990: 38.

Avins, Mimi. "How to Tell the Players in *Joy Luck Club*." *New York Times*, September 5, 1993: H14.

Bach, Steven. *Final Cut: Dreams and Disaster in the Making of* Heaven's Gate. New York: Morrow, 1985.

Banner, Simon. Interview with Spike Lee. *London Sunday Times*, March 8, 1987.

Barth, Jack. "Praising *Arizona*." *Film Comment*, March-April 1987: 18.

Beer, Amy. "So What's So Special About Specialty Film?" *The Off-Hollywood Report*, September-October 1989: 7.

Benson, Sheila. "The Evolution of Spike Lee." *Los Angeles Times*, July 9, 1989: E28.

————. Review of *sex, lies, and videotape*. *Los Angeles Times*, August 4, 1989: E1.

———. Review of *Stranger Than Paradise*. *Los Angeles Times*, November 2, 1984: E18.

———. Review of *Working Girls*. *Los Angeles Times,* March 13, 1987: E1.

Bernard, Jami. Review of *Roger & Me*. *New York Post*, September 27, 1989: 23.

Breitbart, Eric. Interview with Joel and Ethan Coen. *American Film*, May 1985: 4.

Black, Kent. "A Man and His Myth." *Los Angeles Times*. February 1995: E5.

Borden, Lizzie. "Grass-roots Filmmaking." In *Making Movies*, edited by John Russo. New York: Fireside, 1989.

Brown, Georgia. Review of *Roger & Me*. *Village Voice*, December 26, 1989: 102.

———. Review of *sex, lies, and videotape*. *Village Voice*, August 8, 1989: 55.

Brownworth, Victoria A. "Working Girl." *The Advocate*, August 23, 1994: 82.

Brunette, Peter. Review of *Working Girls*. *Film Quarterly*, Winter 1986–87: 54–56.

Bugbee, Victoria. "*Stranger Than Paradise*." *American Cinematographer*, March 1985: 46.

Calvert, Catherine. "The Directors." *Town & Country*, May 1988: 172–73.

Canby, Vincent. "Film: *Chan is Missing* in Chinatown." *New York Times*, April 24, 1982: B1.

———. "Film View: Unexpected Dividends at a Festival." *New York Times*, May 2, 1982: C1.

———. "Rejoice! It's Independents' Day." *New York Times*, October 8, 1989: B1.

Christensen, Terry. *Reel Politics: American Political Movies from* Birth of a Nation *to* Platoon. New York: Basil Blackwell, 1987.

Chute, David. "Designated Writer: An Interview with John Sayles." *Film Comment*, May–June 1981: 54–59.

Cockburn, Alexander. Interview with Michael Moore. *Grand Street*, Winter 1995: 35–46.

Cook, David A. *A History of Narrative Film*. New York: Norton, 1981.

Cook, Pam. Review of *sex, lies, and videotape*. *Monthly Film Bulletin*, September 1989: 282.

Corliss, Richard. "Calling Their Own Shots: Women Directors Are Starting to Make It in Hollywood." *Time*, March 24, 1986: 82–83.

———. Review of *Blood Simple*. *Time*, January 28, 1985: 90.

———. Review of *Smithereens*. *Time*, March 14, 1983: 90.

Corrigan, Timothy. *A Cinema Without Walls: Movies and Culture After Vietnam*. New Brunswick, NJ: Rutgers, 1991.

Cowie, Peter. *Coppola*. New York: Scribner, 1990.

The Criterion Collection: sex, lies, and videotape. Interview with Steven Soderbergh. Santa Monica, CA: Voyager, 1990.

Crouch, Stanley. "Do the Race Thing: Spike Lee's Afro-Fascist Chic." *Village Voice*, June 20, 1989: 73.

Davis, Thulani. "Blue-Collar Auteur." *American Film*, June 1991: 18.

———. "We've Gotta Have It: Spike Lee and a New Black Cinema." *Village Voice*, June 20, 1989: 67.

Dayton, Elyse. Review of *Smithereens. Cineaste* 13, no. 1 (1983): 25.

Deickmann, Katherine. "Liar, Liar, Pants on Fire: Steve Soderbergh Comes Clean." *Village Voice*, August 8, 1989: 32.

Denby, David. Review of *Blood Simple. New York*, January 21, 1985: 51.

———. Review of *Roger & Me. New York*, December 18, 1989: 102.

———. Review of *Roger & Me. New York*, January 29, 1990: 58.

———. Review of *sex, lies, and videotape. New York*, August 7, 1989: 40.

———. Review of *Smithereens. New York*, January 17, 1983: 80.

Dreyfus, Claudia. Interview with John Sayles. *The Progressive*, November 1991: 30.

Duffy, Karen. "The Moore, the Merrier." *Interview*, September 1994: 70.

Dutka, Elaine. "Will Controversy Cost *Roger* an Oscar?" *Los Angeles Times*, January 17, 1990: F1.

———. "Tyro in the Land of the Titans." *Los Angeles Times*, November 4, 1989: F10.

Ebert, Roger. "Taking a Closer Look at Independence." *The Off-Hollywood Report*, November-December 1988: 8.

Edelstein, David. "Invasion of the Baby Snatchers: Joel and Ethan Coen's *Raising Arizona*." *American Film*, April 1987: 26.

———. Review of *Roger & Me. New York Post*, December 20, 1989: 26.

Emerson, Jim "Moore's Dream & *Roger & Me*." *Orange County Register*, January 2, 1990: F5.

Farnsworth, Clyde H. " 'So Long, Flint, Hello, Toronto' A Director Goes Hollywood (North)." *New York Times*, December 13, 1993: C1.

"Film School Generation." *American Cinema*. Public Broadcasting System, KCET, Los Angeles, April 23, 1995.

French, Lisa. "Lizzie Borden's Cutting Edge." *The Off-Hollywood Report*, Fall 1991: 30–32.

Friend, Tad. "Inside the Coen Heads." *Vogue*, April 1994: 348.

Fuller, Graham. Review of *Working Girls. Cineaste* XV, no. 3 (1987): 42.

Fusco, Coco. Interview with Lizzie Borden. *Afterimage*, Fall 1987: 46.

Gabriel, Trip. "Steven Soderbergh: The Sequel." *New York Times Biographical Service*, November 1991: 1166.

Gallagher, John Andrew. *Film Directors on Directing*. New York: Greenwood Press, 1989.

Geist, Kenneth. Review of *Blood Simple. Films in Review*, May 1985: 304.

Gelmis, Joseph. "*Chan is Missing*, and So Are the Cliches." *Newsday*, May 2, 1982: B1.

————. Review of *Chan is Missing*. *Newsday*. April 23, 1982: A22.

Goldstein, Patrick. "Spring Sayles on TV." *Interview*, May 5, 1990: 23.

————. "Sayles on TV." *Interview*, March 1990: 42.

Goodwin, Michael, and Naomi Wise. *On the Edge: The Life & Times of Francis Coppola*. New York: Morrow, 1989.

Grant, Edmond. Review of *sex, lies, and videotape*. *Films in Review*, October 1989: 482.

Greenberg, James. "Sex, Lies, and Kafka." *Connoiseur*, October 1991: 58.

Handelman, David. "Insight to Riot: Director Spike Lee's *Do the Right Thing* Takes a Provocative Look at Race Relations." *Rolling Stone*, July 13, 1989: 104.

————. "The Brothers from Another Planet." *Rolling Stone*, May 21, 1987: 59–64.

Hickenlooper, George. *Reel Conversations: Candid Interviews with Film's Foremost Directors and Critics*. New York: Citadel, 1991.

Hinson, Hal. "Bloodlines." *Film Comment*, March-April 1985: 14–19.

Hoberman, J. Review of *Stranger than Paradise*. *Village Voice*, October 2, 1984: 49.

————. "Get Ready for the New Americanarama." *Premiere*, October 1988: 114–5.

————. "I am a Camera." *Premiere*, January 1990: 37–38.

————. "*Night of the Living Dead* at Twenty." *Premiere*, December 1988: 142–43.

————. Review of *Blood Simple*. *Village Voice*, January 22, 1985: 53.

————. Review of *Roger & Me*. *Village Voice*, October 3, 1989: 61.

————. Review of *Working Girls*. *Village Voice*, March 10, 1987: 54.

————. *Vulgar Modernism: Writing on Movies and Other Media*. Philadelphia: Temple University Press, 1991.

Horowitz, Mark. "Coen Brothers A-Z: The Big Two-Headed Picture." *Film Comment*, September-October 1991.

Hsiao, Andy. "The Man On a 'Joy Luck' Ride: Asian-American Director Wayne Wang, at Home with Women & Tradition." *Washington Post*, September 27, 1993: B1.

Hulser, Kathleen. "Ten Cheap Movies and How They Got That Way." *American Film*, May 1984: 22.

Insdorf, Annette. "*Smithereens*—The Story of a Cinderella Movie." *New York Times*, May 8, 1982: B1.

Iwata, Edward. "Asian Movies Take Flight: Asian-American Directors and Films Move into Mainstream." *Los Angeles Times*, May 13, 1993: F1.

Jacobson, Harlan. "John Sayles's Committed Cinema." *Interview*, April 1993: 113.

————. "Michael and Me: A Leader on the Left Meets a Follower of the Left Behind." *Film Comment*, November-December 1989: 16.

————. "Three Guys in Three Directions; *Stranger than Paradise*: $120,000." *Film Comment*, February 1985: 60.

————. "Truth or Consequences: Steven Soderbergh, King of Cannes." *Film Comment*, July-August 1989: 22–28.

Jaehne, Karen. Review of *sex, lies, and videotape. Cineaste* 17, no. 3 (1990): 38.

James, David E. *Allegories of Cinema: American Film in the Sixties*. Princeton: Princeton University Press, 1989.

Jenkins, Steve. Review of *Blood Simple. Monthly Film Bulletin*, January 1985: 19.

Jost, Jon. "End of the Indies: Death of the Sayles Men." *Film Comment*, January-February 1989: 42–45.

Jowett, Garth. *Film: The Demomcratic Art*. Boston: Little, Brown, 1981.

Kael, Pauline. Review of *Roger & Me. The New Yorker*, January 8, 1990: 84.

Kaleta, Kenneth C. *David Lynch*. New York: Twain, 1992.

Kaufman, Bill. Review of *Smithereens. Newsday*, November 19, 1982: II6.

Kaufman, Michael T. "In a New Film, Spike Lee Tries To Do the Right Thing." *The New York Times*, June 25, 1989: B1+.

Kelleher, Terry. Review of *Roger & Me. Newsday*, September 27, 1989: II5.

Klein, Joe. "You Can't Get There From Here: The Spirit of the Sixties Has Escaped the Camera as Cruelly as It Has Eluded the Fading Flower Children—With *The Big Chill*, Lawrence Kasdan Hopes to Tell It Like It Is." *American Film*, October 1983: 40.

Kramer, Mimi. "Undressed for Success: For Today's Yuppie Hookers, Prostitution is Just One of the Better Career Options." *Vogue*, July 1987: 218.

Lardner, Jr., Ring. "Foul Ball: John Sayles's *Eight Men Out*—Or, How My Father Watched the White Sox Throw the 1919 World Series." *American Film*, July-August 1988: 45.

Lee, Spike. *Spike Lee's Gotta Have It: Inside Guerrilla Filmmaking*. New York: Simon and Schuster, 1987.

Levin, Doron P. "Michael Moore: Tweaking the Captains of Industry in Prime Time." *New York Times Biographical Service*, July 1994: 1043–44.

Levitt, Shelley. "John Sayles." *People Weekly*, March 8, 1993: 86.

Lewis, Jon. *The Road to Romance and Ruin: Teen Films and Youth Culture*. New York: Routledge, 1992.

Loeb, Anthony, ed. *Filmmakers in Conversation*. Chicago: Columbia College, 1982.

Loud, Lance. "Jim Jarmusch Takes a Shortcut." *American Film*, January 1990: 16.

Marchese, John. "Me: The Continuing Adventures of Michael Moore." *Esquire*, January 1993: 44.

Maslin, Janet. Review of *The Joy Luck Club*. *New York Times*, September 8, 1993: B1.

———. Interview with Susan Seidelman. *The New York Times*, March 22, 1985: C1.

Mathews, Jack. "Controversial Film for a Long Hot Summer." *Los Angeles Times*, May 22, 1989:VI5.

Mayer, Ira. Review of *Smithereens*. *New York Post*, November 19, 1982: 43.

McCarthy, Todd, and Charles Flynn. Eds. *Kings of the B's*. New York: Dutton, 1975.

McCarty, John. *Modern Horror Film*. New York: Citadel, 1990.

———. *Splatter Films: Breaking the Last Taboo of the Screen*. New York: St. Martin's, 1984.

McDonald, Scott. *A Critical Cinema 2: Interviews with Independent Filmmakers*. Berkeley: University of California Press, 1992.

———. *A Critical Cinema: Interviews with Independent Filmmakers*. Berkeley: University of California Press, 1988.

McGhee, Dorothy. "Solidarity Forever: In an Era of Union-Busting, John Sayles's *Matewan* Celebrates the Miners' Struggles of the Twenties." *American Film*, September 1987: 42.

Minsky, Terri. "Hot Phenom: Hollywood Makes a Big Deal Over Steven Soderbergh's *sex, lies, and videotape*." *Rolling Stone*, May 18, 1989: 85.

———. "Sayles and Bargains." *Premiere*, September 1991: 38.

———. "The Feminine Mystique (Story on *She-Devil*)." *Premiere*, December 1989: 76.

Moore, Michael. "Michael and IFP: Slated for Success?" *The Off-Hollywood Report* November-December 1989: 18–19.

Moore, Suzanne. Review of *Roger & Me*. *New Statesman & Society*, April 27, 90: 48.

———. Review of *sex, lies, and videotape*. *New Statesman & Society*, September 15, 1989: 44.

Morrone, John. Review of *sex, lies, and videotape*. New Leader, October 2–16, 1989: 20.

Mott, Donald. *Steven Spielberg*. New York: Twayne, 1986.

Nangle, John. Review of *Smithereens*. *Films in Review*, January 1983: 51.

Osborne, David. "John Sayles: From Hoboken to Hollywood—And Back." *American Film*, October 1982: 30.

Pall, Ellen. "Sets Big and Small Challenge Movie Makers; *Night on Earth*: Was Filming Inside a Cab a Deadly Trap?" *New York Times*, June 7, 1992: H13.

Pally, Marcia. "Closely Watched Train: Jarmusch's Triptych to Ride." *Film Comment*. July-August 1989: 19–21.

Patterson, Richard. "*Chan is Missing*, Or How to Make a Successful Feature for $22,315.92." *American Cinematographer*, February 1983: 32–39.

––––––. "An Interview with Susan Seidelman on the Making of *Smithereens*." *American Cinematographer*, May 1983: 68–70, 123–26.

Peary, Danny. *Cult Movies 3: Fifty More of the the Classics, the Sleepers, the Weird, and the Wonderful*. New York: Fireside, 1988.

––––––. *Cult Movies 2: Fifty More of the the Classics, the Sleepers, the Weird, and the Wonderful*. New York: Dell, 1983.

Pitman, Randy. Review of *Chan is Missing*. *Library Journal*, January 1990: 164.

Pollock, Dale. *Skywalking: The Life and Films of George Lucas*. New York: Crown, 1983.

Pooley, Eric. "Warped in America: The Dark Vision of Moviemakers Joel and Ethan Coen." *New York*, March 23, 1987: 44–48.

Quart, Barbara Koenig. *Women Directors: The Emergence of a New Cinema*. New York: Praeger, 1988.

Rainer, Peter. Review of *Roger & Me*. *Los Angeles Times*, December 20, 1989: E1.

Richardson, John H. "The Joel and Ethan Story." *Premiere*, October 1990: 94.

Rickey, Carrie. "Some Moving Pictures (and Some That Aren't)" *Village Voice*, April 27, 1982: 27.

––––––. "Where the Girls Are." *American Film*, January-February 1984: 48.

Robertson, William Preston. "The Coen Brothers Made Easy." *American Film*, August 1991: 30+.

Rohter, Larry. Interview with Spike Lee. *New York Times*, August 10, 1986.

Interview with Spike Lee. *Rolling Stone*, July 13, 1989: 107.

Rose, Cynthia. Review of *Smithereens*. *Monthly Film Bulletin*, March 1983: 75.

Rosen, David, with Peter Hamilton. *Off-Hollywood: The Making and Marketing of American Independent Films*. New York: Grove Weidenfeld, 1990.

Rosenbaum, Ron. "Movies on the Make." *Mademoiselle*, August 1992: 58–59.

Sante, Luc. "The Rise of the Baroque Directors." *Vogue*, September 1992: 321.

––––––. "Mystery Man." *Interview*, November 1989: 146.

Sarris, Andrew. "Baby, It's You: An Honest Man Becomes a True Filmmaker." *Film Comment*, May-June 1993: 28.

––––––. Review of *Smithereens*. *Village Voice*, November 30, 1982: 59.

Sayles, John. *Thinking in Pictures: The Making of the Movie* Matewan.

Schickel, Richard. Review of *Roger & Me*. *Time*, January 8, 1990: 77.

Schlesinger, T. "Putting People Together: An Interview with John Sayles." *Film Quarterly*, Summer 1981: 2–8.

Schneider, Wolf. "More from Moore." *American Film*. July 1990: 24.

Schoemer, Karen. "A Director's Night on Earth, Close to Home." *New York Times*, May 1, 1992: B1.

————. "Film as Life, and Vice Versa." *New York Times*, April 30, 1992: C1.

Seligsohn, Leo. Review of *Stranger than Paradise*. *Newsday*, September 28, 1984: II6.

Shapiro, Jame. Interview with Jim Jarmusch. *Village Voice*, September 16, 1986.

Sklar, Robert. *Film: An International History of the Medium*. New York: Abrams, 1994.

Smith, Craig S. "A Rare Shot at Screen Stardom for Asians." *Wall Street Journal*, September 1, 1992: A12.

Soderbergh, Steven. *sex, lies, and videotape*. New York: Harper and Row, 1990.

Spheeris, Penelope. "Western Civilization Declines Again." *Premiere*, June 1988: 112.

Stam, Robert. *New Vocabularies in Film Semiotics: Structuralism, Post-structuralism and Beyond*. New York: Routledge, 1992.

Stark, Jim. "Garage Movies: Part I." *The Off-Hollywood Report*, July-August 1990: 12.

Sterritt, David. Review of *Roger & Me*. *Christian Science Monitor*, January 16, 1990: 10.

————. Review of *Smithereens*. *Christian Science Monitor*, December 9, 1982: 18.

————. Review of *Stranger Than Paradise*. *Christian Science Monitor*, October 4, 1984: 25.

Stone, Judy. "A Humorous Treat From Chinatown." *San Francisco Chronicle*, December 12, 1981: B3.

Tajima, Renee. "The Perils of Popularity." *The Independent*, June 1990: 29–31.

Thomas, Kenneth. "*Secaucus Seven*: Low Budget, High Rating." November 5, 1980: D1+.

Thomas, Kevin. Review of *Smithereens*. *Los Angeles Times*, January 13, 1983: E1.

Thompson, Ben. "Sex, Lies and Urban Renewal." *New Statesman & Society*, November 15, 1991: 37.

Thomson, David. "Chinese Takeout: Wayne Wang Interviewed." *Film Comment*, September-October 1985: 23.

Travers, Peter. Rev. of *Life is Cheap...but Toilet Paper is Expensive*, by Wayne Wang. *Rolling Stone*, September 20, 1990: 48.

Van Gelder, Lawrence. Interview with Jim Jarmusch. *The New York Times*, October 21, 1984: B4.

Vineberg, Steve. *No Surprises, Please: Movies in the Reagan Decade*. New York: Schirmer, 1993.

Walker, Beverly. "The Disappearing Director." *American Film*, January-February 1989: 28.

"Views From the Edge." *American Cinema*. Public Broadcasting System, KCET, Los Angeles, April 30, 1995.

Weinraub, Bearnard. "I Didn't Want To Do Another Chinese Movie." *New York Times*, September 5, 993: H7.

White, Armond. "Birth of a Nation: Spike Lee Shows the Limits of Intolerance." *LA Weekly*, July 7, 1989: 31.

Williamson, Judith. Review of *Working Girls. New Statesman*, March 20, 1987: 26.

Wilmington, Michael. "Director Puts Much Value on Tough-Sell Reputation." *Los Angeles Times*, Febuary 27, 1990: F2.

———. "Delicate Cultural Flavor in *Bowl of Tea*." *Los Angleles Times*, August 5, 1989: F14.

———. Review of *Mystery Train. Los Angeles Times*, December 20, 1989: F6.

Wilson, David. Review of *Roger & Me. Monthly Film Bulletin*, April 1990: 116.

Wong, Wayman. "A Mystery Movie is Actually Much More." *The San Francisco Examiner*, December 10, 1981: C2.

Zavarzadeh, Mas'ud. *Seeing Films Politically*. Albany: SUNY Press, 1991.

Index

About the Author

RICHARD K. FERNCASE is Associate Professor of Film and Television at Chapman University in Southern California.

ISBN 0-313-27607-2

HARDCOVER BAR CODE